Boyce Thompson

DESIGNING
FOR DISASTER

DOMESTIC ARCHITECTURE IN THE ERA OF CLIMATE CHANGE

SCHIFFER
PUBLISHING

4880 Lower Valley Road • Atglen, PA 19310

Other Schiffer Books by Boyce Thompson:

Anatomy of a Great Home, ISBN 978-0-7643-5465-6

Copyright © 2019 by Boyce Thompson

Library of Congress Control Number: 2019936851

Designed by Molly Shields
Front cover: Joe Fletcher Photography
Back cover: Robert Benson Photography

Type set in Rockwell/ZapfEllipt BT

ISBN: 978-0-7643-5784-8
Printed in China

Published by Schiffer Publishing, Ltd.
4880 Lower Valley Road
Atglen, PA 19310
Phone: (610) 593-1777; Fax: (610) 593-2002
E-mail: Info@schifferbooks.com
Web: www.schifferbooks.com

For our complete selection of fine books on this and related subjects, please visit our website at www.schifferbooks.com. You may also write for a free catalog.

Schiffer Publishing's titles are available at special discounts for bulk purchases for sales promotions or premiums. Special editions, including personalized covers, corporate imprints, and excerpts, can be created in large quantities for special needs. For more information, contact the publisher.

We are always looking for people to write books on new and related subjects. If you have an idea for a book, please contact us at proposals@schifferbooks.com.

CONTENTS

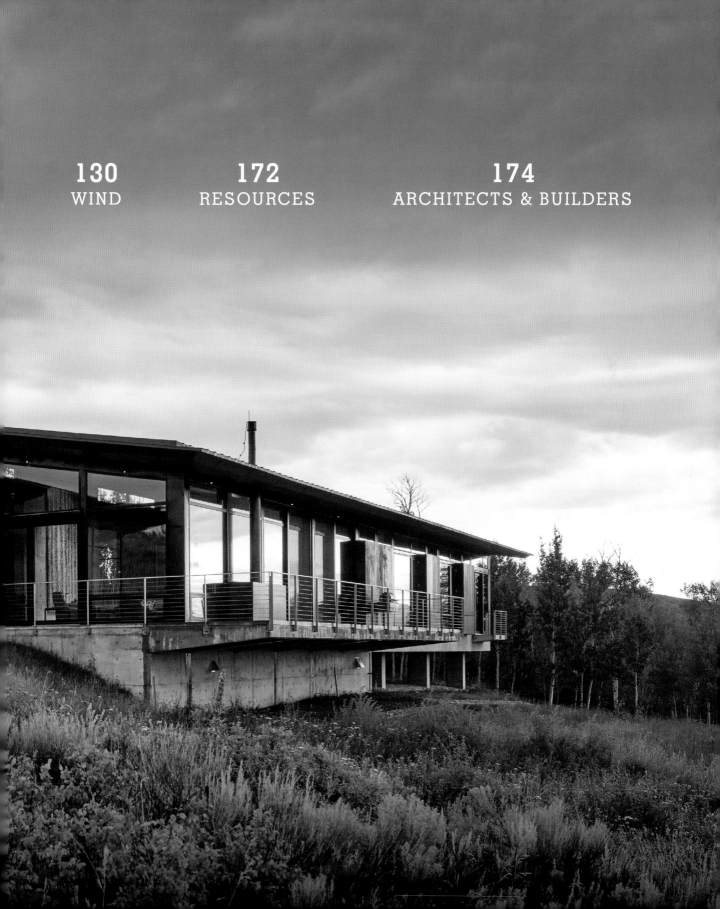

THE MOST PRUDENT PATH
IS A PROACTIVE ONE.

INTRO DUCTION

The need for adequate shelter has taken on a new urgency. Homes have always had to resist the debilitating natural forces of floodwaters, driving winds, sweeping wildfires, and shifting earth. But extreme weather events brought on by climate change have raised the stakes. As the planet warms, incidents that were supposed to happen only once in a hundred years—devastating hurricanes, deadly tornadoes, and wildfires burning out of control—occur with alarming frequency. To design and build a home that resists natural forces, one that will last for generations, requires far-deeper understanding of how a worsening environment impacts home design.

The National Academy of Sciences links the increased occurrence and severity of weather events to global warming. Its bellwether 2014 report, *Climate Change: Evidence and Causes*, noted that as carbon emissions increase, the

The Great Northern California fires skipped from forests into urban areas, burning entire neighborhoods, like this one in Santa Rosa. *Photo courtesy of FEMA*

earth's lower atmosphere warms, creating "the potential for more energy for storms and certain severe weather events. Consistent with theoretical expectations, heavy rainfall and snowfall events (which increase the risk of flooding) and heat waves are generally becoming more frequent" in North America and parts of Europe. It's more difficult for the academy to link hurricanes and tornadoes to global warming; they are by definition rare and affected by natural climate variations. But the organization notes that they too are increasing in intensity.

The seas absorb more than 90 percent of the excess heat retained by greenhouse gases. As they warm—their temperature has increased 1.5 degrees F in the last century—waters rise and coastal communities flood. The worst is yet to come. The National Ocean and Atmospheric Agency (NOAA) predicts that sea levels will rise a foot or two within the next thirty years, and 8 feet in the worst case by 2100. They may rise higher if Greenland and Antarctica continue to melt faster than expected. One in ten Florida homes could be underwater by the turn of the century, according to the Union of Concerned Scientists. Big swaths of New Jersey and New York could be submerged. Rising seas may overwhelm cities such as Norfolk and New Orleans that are sinking anyway.

The sobering news is that not much can be done to prevent severe weather from becoming more common. The shift in the earth's temperature started with the Industrial Revolution, when human activity preempted a natural cooling cycle. Even if one country gets its act together, the impact of lax standards is felt around the world—carbon emissions generated anywhere on the planet mix in the atmosphere within a year. The bottom line is that during the lifetime of any home built today, the planet will warm, the seas will rise, and severe weather events will proliferate. In the United States, hundred-year storms occur so frequently that people forget their names.

A house built to last fifty years has at least a 50 percent chance of being victimized by a major storm. Put another way, there's a one-in-a-hundred chance that a hundred-year event will happen in any given year. And, as recent events have shown, there's no reason why megastorms can't happen two years in a row. Ellicott City, Maryland, got hit with two hundred-year storms within three years. Hurricane Harvey was Houston's third 500-year flood in three years. When Hurricane Florence followed on the heels of Matthew, it was the second hundred-year flood in North Carolina in three years. The wide swath of flooding proved FEMA's published flood maps to be woefully out of date.

The mounting threat has birthed the practice of "resilient" design. The goal: build homes to stand up to, and rebound from, extreme weather conditions. The movement is local by nature; homes in Big Sur are more vulnerable to earthquakes and mudslides than homes in Oklahoma City. At the same time, some of the precautions taken during design and construction can protect homes from multiple threats. That's the case with coastal hurricane-safety techniques such as lateral wall bracing and foundation anchors, which also prevent tornado damage in the Midwest. Similarly, a moment frame—where structural elements are tied together so that they move as one unit—defends against both earthquakes and massive storm surges.

That said, there's only so much you can do to escape the wrath of a major landslide or an EF5 tornado. It's hard for any oceanfront home, even one suspended well above the floodplain, to survive the onslaught of a category 4 hurricane; news footage of towns decimated by Hurricane Matthew along the Florida Gulf

Flooding caused by heavy rains and snowmelt laid waste to the town of Jamestown, Colorado, taking out homes near a stream. The flooding occurred after wildfires denuded the surrounding hills. *Photo courtesy of FEMA*

coast certainly proved that. The eye of the tornado that ripped through Joplin, Missouri, in 2011 left nothing but rubble in its wake, even flattening hospitals and schools built with masonry and steel. Wildfires that ravaged Northern California in 2017 skipped into urban areas, destroying entire subdivisions.

Resilient design focuses instead on preventing the lion's share of disaster damage. Most havoc wreaked by tornadoes—about 90 percent, according to forensic engineers—is caused by winds outside the core of big twisters, or by storms that are not particularly severe. Tying the roof to the walls and the walls to the foundation, installing impact-resistant glass, and beefing up garage doors reduce the potential for most damage. Similarly, wildfires may bypass homes without flammable

vegetation around the perimeter, especially if vents are screened so that flying embers can't get inside and the roof and walls are built with noncombustible materials.

The easy response to resilient design is to design big, windowless concrete bunkers. Indeed, several early demonstration homes ignore aesthetics and livability in pursuit of safety. But the requirements needn't be mutually exclusive. You should be able to open windows and enjoy sea breezes in an oceanfront home, and to close them securely when storms threaten. You should be able to watch cottonwoods bend in the breeze from your riverside home—even if the banks periodically overflow. A country retreat needs to embrace the woods even as it keeps the trees at a distance. The homes in this book show that the

Hurricane Sandy destroyed or damaged 650,000 homes in the Northeast, lifting some from their foundations. *Photo courtesy of FEMA*

River flooding brought on by Hurricane Matthew submerged western Craven County, North Carolina. *Photo courtesy of FEMA*

needs of resiliency, aesthetics, and livability can work in harmony.

The most resilient homes not only resist extreme natural forces but can bounce back from them. Their systems may operate independent of the utility grid. Several homes in the book produce drinking water from rain. Most are designed to circulate cool breezes when electricity isn't available to run air conditioning. Others include awnings and overhangs to prevent harsh summer sun from overheating living spaces, so that homes may not even need air conditioning. All of them do their best not to contribute to the carbon emissions that brought on climate change in the first place, even though no single home can make a difference at this point.

Increasingly, resiliency is a pocketbook matter. A Harvard University study found that in particularly vulnerable places—the shorelines of Miami and New Jersey, for instance—home values aren't keeping pace with the market. Some coastal neighborhoods flood with such regularity now that local governments, to the dismay of residents trying to sell their homes,

The 2014 Oso, Washington, mudslide, one of the deadliest in US history, destroyed forty-nine buildings and took forty-three lives. Logging may have contributed to the hill's instability. *Photo courtesy of FEMA*

post signs warning of the corrosive effects of seawater on parked cars. The desire to protect home values—the dominant form of wealth for most families—has touched off a groundswell movement to improve public infrastructure—waterways and sewer systems in particular.

Unfortunately, most homeowner insurance policies don't cover flooding, the most common and costly natural disaster in the United States. Most homeowners, though, can buy flood insurance from FEMA for an average of $58 a month. Coverage tops out at $250,000 for a structure and at $100,000 for possessions. Mortgage lenders typically require owners of homes within the FEMA-designated hundred-year floodplain to carry the insurance. The problem is that people living outside the zone may not know their house stands in harm's way.

FEMA, tasked with updating its maps every five years, isn't keeping up with climate change. A recent government report by the Department of Homeland Security's Inspector General's Office found that only 42 percent of the agency's maps accurately represent flood threats. One reason for the slow pace: communities resist redesignation out of fear it may lower property values.

Local building codes, which primarily focus on making sure buildings don't collapse and that you can escape if they do, aren't keeping pace with changing weather patterns, either. Model building codes, on which local codes are based, may address the growing threats, but local governments are slow to adopt them. Big natural disasters often lead to calls to action to protect homes from floods, tornadoes, hurricanes, or wildfires. Sometimes government officials respond to the pressure, but in most cases political entropy sets in. Builders may successfully lobby that the changes will make new homes too expensive. Even if new protections are adopted, they may be weakened down the road as the memory of tragic events fades.

Protections that do work their way into codes are a good place to turn for guidance. Examples include Florida's hurricane standards; the tornado code for Moore, Oklahoma; California's earthquake provisions; and Colorado's fire-safe requirements. Published voluntary guidelines for hurricane-, earthquake-, fire-, and tornado-safe homes are worth checking out as well—they are often developed by insurers looking to limit losses. And the nation's model building codes, widely available online for those who don't mind wading through technical literature, often have the most up-to-date protections.

It's up to homeowners, working closely with their architects and builders, to ensure that their house is built to last. Even in places where codes provide protection from hurricanes or tornadoes, they may not be thoroughly enforced. In the wake of Hurricane Andrew, engineers discovered many recent-vintage South Florida homes that ignored local hurricane codes. Katrina, the Big One feared for decades in the Big Easy, exposed the common practice of obtaining building approvals over a liquid lunch. The growing frequency of severe weather events throughout the country makes it more difficult to ignore the lessons of the past. More and more cities, designers, and homeowners are deciding that the most prudent path is a proactive one.

Four hundred thousand people were displaced from New Orleans after Hurricane Katrina exposed fatal flaws in the city's flood protection system. *Photo courtesy of FEMA*

Hibiscus Island House. *Photo courtesy of Choeff Levy Fischman*

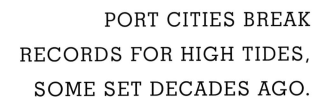

WATER

Miami, pictured on these pages, is ground zero for global warming in the United States. If nothing changes, large swaths of the city will be underwater by the turn of the century. Homes along the inland waterway, with no beaches for protection, are in greatest jeopardy. It's not just rising seas that make them vulnerable; storm surges and tidal flooding will take their toll as well. High-tide flooding has doubled in the last thirty years, according a NOAA study of nearly a hundred locations relying on tide gauges that have been in place for a century or so. The pace is accelerating; it grew 50 percent in last eight years.

Tidal floods used to be rare in Annapolis, Maryland, on the Chesapeake Bay. But now, nearly forty days a year, nuisance flooding threatens homes, closes harbor restaurants, deters tourists, and ultimately costs jobs. Within the next fifty years, according to NOAA projections, parts of Annapolis can expect to flood at least once a day. In the meantime, the city recommends that homeowners in harm's way elevate their homes, install flood vents, grade lots so that water flows away from the house, install sump pumps in crawl spaces, and patch foundation walls. Meanwhile, the government is repairing sidewalks to create a clear path for floodwater to pass and upgrading its sewer system so that it's less likely to back up during storms and high tides.

Even without the push of a flood, water insidiously works its way inside a home. It discovers gaps in roof sheathing, zeroes in on poor window flashing, or bubbles up from beneath the basement. Sometimes it works subtly—condensation builds up behind walls until black mold finally appears or drywall crumbles. During big storms, high winds can lift roofs from their mooring, toss siding around the neighborhood, and crack measly windows. Then demon water wends its way inside, ruining interiors. Insurers say that mold can grow on a damp surface within one to two days. Insurance can't cover the loss of marriage photos, heirloom furniture, and your children's art projects.

Big snowstorms are a symptom of the same problem, according to NOAA. A warmer atmosphere holds more water vapor, the fuel for snow. Northern regions where snow is common can expect heavier snowfalls for that reason.

Twice as many snowstorms hit the eastern two-thirds of the country in the second half of the twentieth century compared to the first. High ocean surface temperatures from El Niño currents worsen the situation. In 2010, warmer-than-normal seas contributed to "snomaggedon," a monster storm that dumped 17.8 inches of snow on unsuspecting Washington, DC.

Meanwhile, port cities break records for high tides, some set decades ago. Charleston, South Carolina, recently exceeded the tidal surge of a 1928 hurricane four times in one year. Boston and Atlantic City now have twenty-two days a year when seawater inundates infrastructure. The Embarcadero in San Francisco, built safely above sea level 150 years ago, now floods twenty days a year. The situation worsens as hurricanes bring storm surges that wipe away the coastline. The evidence suggests that today's storm surges become tomorrow's high-tide levels.

PARADISE REVISITED

Hibiscus Island House

Miami, Florida

Choeff Levy Fischman

6,000 square feet

A seawall is a first line of defense for the Hibiscus House, precariously situated along Miami's inland waterway. *Photos courtesy of Choeff Levy Fischman*

Who doesn't dream of spending idyllic afternoons sipping fruity cocktails under palm trees beside a disappearing-edge pool with Jobim playing from hidden speakers? Unfortunately, today's dream of owning a home in a tropical paradise needs to be tempered by the reality of severe weather: homes must resist the party-spoiling threats of hurricanes, storm surges, and rising sea levels. Otherwise, as Floridians learned the hard way during tropical storms Andrew, Irma, and Matthew, dreams become nightmares and sometimes even lead to financial ruin.

The stakes were high for Hibiscus Island House, designed by the Miami-based architecture firm Choeff Levy Fischman. Its spectacular setting—on man-made Hibiscus Island, surrounded by Biscayne Bay—makes it particularly vulnerable to the elements. With little protection against storm surges, the island is among the first places to be evacuated when hurricanes threaten South Florida. Architects like to think their buildings will remain standing long after they pass, a testament to the prescience of their work. The future impacts of global warming make that noble goal trickier to achieve.

A seawall that rises 7.26 feet above sea level provides an important first line of defense for the vulnerable house. To further buffer it from storm surges, the architects sited the home 22 to 26 feet from the shoreline.

Additional security comes from elaborate grade changes designed to mitigate neighborhood street flooding. A series of limestone pavers elegantly rises through the front yard to meet the house, which sits 10 feet above sea level. The path culminates in an up-close view of a two-story glass stairwell tower.

Pocket sliding doors, disappearing corners, and large glass-plate windows open the house to its tropical surroundings. Large overhangs provide sanctuary for outdoor living during the rainy season.

Limestone floors, white ceilings, and disappearing doors blur the boundary between the living room and the patio.

The house's foundation, floors, and roof were formed in one integrated pour, eliminating the need for connectors that might fail in a severe storm.

The home's roost presented another challenge: controlling runoff. The solution was to build retaining walls that preserve rainwater to keep the lot from eroding. The walls work with a series of trenches and drains that capture and filter water. The system comes in handy when floods cut off potable water supplies; it produces water clean enough for drinking, bathing, washing clothes, and doing dishes. (FEMA recommends keeping a supply of potable water in homes vulnerable to flooding—one gallon per day per person.)

The high winds that accompany driving rain called for additional protections. The architects framed the house with rows of concrete blocks, reinforced intermittently with rebar and poured concrete. Its foundation, floors, and roof were formed in one integrated concrete pour, eliminating the need for connectors. During a storm, a home is only as strong as its weakest link, and that's usually the windows and doors. On this house they were made with category 5 hurricane–resistant glass and frames that can withstand the pressure of 150-mile-per-hour winds and the impact of flying debris.

The Hibiscus Island house was also designed to endure the everyday Florida

The front walk rises with the sloped lot to a dynamic, glass-lined, two-story entry perched above neighborhood flood levels.

hazards of rainy seasons, dry winters, and intense summer heat, a particularly big challenge given the many glass walls. Carefully calibrated low-e film in windows and patio doors minimizes solar heat gain and glare. A light-colored "cool" roof—it absorbs less heat than a dark one—reflects sunlight back into the sky, reducing air conditioning needs during intense summer heat. In more-comfortable seasons, ceiling fans circulate cool air through an open floor plan.

Sliding glass doors open both levels of the house to the tropical environment. The corner of the living room disappears, thanks to column-free sliders that pocket into walls to produce uninterrupted views of the Miami skyline. The master bedroom appears to float over a shaded pool with a cascading fountain and stone accents. Doors in the master bath open to create the opportunity for al fresco bathing in a large

soaking tub. Even in the second-floor office, patio doors open to sea air.

Surfaces run from inside to outside to link the environments. Limestone floors extend from the great room to an expansive patio. Cumaru, a resilient Brazilian hardwood used to clad the exterior walls, makes a return appearance in the great room and master bedroom. Board-formed concrete was used for walls both outside and inside. To further blur boundaries, the home's interiors and exterior rely on the same basic color palette—white stucco, cumaru, and gray concrete. Wood accents—a bar built from stained Italian oak and Brazilian oak wood floors in the master bedroom suite—warm the modern interiors.

To protect it from high winds that accompany storm surges, the structure is framed with rows of concrete blocks reinforced with rebar and poured concrete.

The home's outdoor architecture more than delivers on the promise of a tropical paradise. On most days, a waterfall set against a poured-concrete wall produces a soothing sound. Underwater lights in the rectangular swimming pool cast intriguing reflections. A sunken, covered entertainment area provides an ideal spot to lounge with family and friends, share a drink, and take in the city lights. Above all, the Hibiscus House offers firm proof that resiliency and great architecture can go hand in hand.

A freestanding soaking tub in the master bath provides a compelling vantage point for enjoying the city skyline.

The resilient exterior combines tropical hardwood, smooth white stucco, and board-formed concrete.

ONE NATION UNDERWATER

During the last housing downturn, economists popularized the term "underwater" to refer to negative equity—the dire situation where homeowners owe more on a mortgage than their home is worth. Now the expression is used to define an even more calamitous condition—homes that may be literally submerged. Zillow, the online index of property values, estimates that if sea levels rise 6 feet by the turn of the century—a conservative forecast—1.9 million homes would wind up underwater, nearly half of them in Florida (www.zillow.com, 2017).

Miami leads the list of large cities at significant risk. It would lose a quarter of its housing stock. But more than one in six Boston homes are also in jeopardy—no surprise considering that a big chunk of the city was built on landfill. New Yorkers, as Hurricane Sandy presaged, may lose 3 percent of their housing stock if the seas climb as predicted. Flooding, the report concludes, would be "especially catastrophic" for lower-income Americans, who spend a disproportionate share of earnings on housing. In Oregon, the bottom price tier accounts for more than half the homes at risk.

In coming decades, tidal flooding—which now typically occurs during high-tide events such as full and new moons—promises to become a near-daily occurrence in some seaside communities. In *Underwater: Rising Seas, Chronic Floods, and the Implications for Coastal Real Estate* (2018), the Union of Concern Scientists (UCS) reports that half a million homes would be chronically inundated by rising sea levels by 2045, with the mid-Atlantic region most at risk. Atlantic City and Cape May, New Jersey, along with Washington, DC, and Wilmington, North Carolina, can expect tidal flooding 240 or more times per year. Pier construction will be much more commonplace. It currently accounts for fewer than 1 percent of homes built nationally.

The report emphasizes the need for cities to update stormwater systems and other public infrastructure to keep up with king tides—the highest and lowest naturally occurring tides. The danger is that residents will abandon communities that are routinely swamped, lowering the tax base and making it even more difficult for communities to pay for infrastructure improvements. Local governments could be caught in a downward economic spiral that wipes out neighborhoods, even if rising sea levels don't. "Some smaller, more rural communities may see 30, 50, or even 70 percent of their property tax revenue at risk due to the number of

chronically inundated homes," says Kristy Dahl, senior climate scientist at UCS and report coauthor. Economists are already finding links between the threat of rising waters and falling property values. Harvard researchers established that properties in low-lying areas of Miami-Dade County, particularly Miami Beach, appreciate slower than others in the metro area. Using Zillow data going back to 1971, they estimate that homes exposed to rising sea levels sell at a 7 percent discount compared to similar properties not subject to climate-related risk (http://iopscience.iop.org, 2018). A University of Colorado review of nearly a half-million homes throughout the country also found that homes vulnerable to rising seas sell at a 7 percent discount (https://papers.ssrn.com, 2017).

High floodwaters remained after Hurricane Matthew.
Photo courtesy of FEMA

RAISED AT THE BEACH

Beach Haven Residence

Long Island Beach, New Jersey

Specht Architects

2,500 square feet

Construction had just begun on the Lofgrens' beach home when Hurricane Sandy hit the Jersey Shore, reducing their oceanfront lot to rubble. The extreme weather event—which created 14-foot storm surges, flooded Manhattan, and caused fires that reduced entire neighborhoods to ash—forced a total redesign of the family's weekend retreat. As it turns out, Craig and Stephanie had plenty of time to mull options. It took three politically contentious years for new building requirements to flow from the calamitous event.

The biggest change made by architect Scott Specht, who had also designed the home that never got built, was to raise it on piers 8 feet above sea level. That adjustment, of course, dramatically decreases the odds that another "hundred-year" storm will wipe out the new

Beach Haven's dark structural undercarriage is deftly integrated into the design and almost disappears from view at sundown. *Photos courtesy of Specht Architects*

Pillars suspend the house 8 feet above sea level. The at-grade garage and storage space have breakout panels that can be washed out by waves without affecting the rest of the house.

house. The aesthetic challenge for Specht was making the piers look like an integral part of the home rather than spindly appendages, a common sight on beach homes up and down the shore. The worst look like boxy flamingoes or mechanical beasts from *Star Wars*, with legs strangely out of proportion to the house's body.

"Our intent was to embrace the fact that the house had to be elevated on what are basically telephone poles driven into the sand, and use them as major design components to be expressed and highlighted," Specht says.

The pillars, stained to match the home's dark cedar walls, form linear colonnades that blend with the starkly modern massing. They support an integrated wood-and-steel frame that cradles the house's main volume. Parts of the home and furnishings that the Lofgrens could part with in the event of high waters—the garage, storage space, and breakout panels—were left at grade. The arrangement means that the next flood, assuming it's not a tsunami, can't reach structural walls that could bring down the house. The family enters at the beach level through a cedar and fiberglass stairwell tucked behind seven of the load-bearing pillars.

Specht borrowed boat-building techniques and materials to design a super-hardy home. Fiberglass, the same material used to build a boat hull, forms the roof. Siding made from stainless steel—also used to protect the sides of a ship from seawater—will stand up to wind-driven rain. Hurricane-resistant windows, an uncommon spec this far north, will take the impact of flying debris, such as wood from a lifeguard chair. Contrasting cedar

A stairwell bump preserves interior floor space and throws light into the main living areas.

cladding—some blanched white, some darkened with a boat stain—gives the home sculptural form. "Cedar has proven over time to be extremely durable in a beach environment," says Specht.

A small lot and government-imposed height and footprint restrictions required thoughtful space allocations. Specht drew a rectilinear form that maximizes the cubic space available on the lot. Then he carved out voids and added balconies and a stairwell bumpout above grade to create visual interest. The stairwell, wrapped with glass on two sides, draws light into the public spaces. With the stairs pulled to one side, a clear line of sight from front to back makes the house appear larger inside. So does full-height glass that invites ocean-gazing from the great room. A large screened panel opposite the stairwell provides privacy from close neighbors.

The need for resiliency doesn't interfere with the ability to create a comfortable retreat. An open plan, with designated zones for living, dining, and food prep, maximizes family time, and a large terrace, open to the living room, is the next best thing to being on the beach. It provides an ideal vantage point to watch the sun rise, waves crash, and hobbyists search for change. A private office provides a refuge when work needs to get done. The guest room is also on the main level, isolated for privacy from the family bedrooms above. When the ocean is too cold for swimming, the Lofgrens can retreat to a hot tub tucked around back on a small deck over the garage.

A large panel covered with gradient wallpaper creates privacy in public rooms. Quirky light fixtures contribute to the relaxed beach vibe.

An eastern orientation means the home benefits from the morning sun and stays cool in the afternoon.

The house's third level is devoted to relaxation and sleep. A fireplace and private terrace overlooking the beach make the master bedroom suite an ideal spot to wind down in the evening. The kids, accustomed to living in a compact Manhattan apartment, were given free rein to customize their bedrooms. The result: an eclectic array of murals, colors, and furnishings. The family can sleep peacefully knowing that the house will withstand much of the water Mother Nature throws their way.

A private terrace off the master bedroom is the perfect place to watch the sun rise or the waves roll in.

BRAD PITT TRIES TO MAKE IT RIGHT

Actor Brad Pitt issued a challenge to architects in the wake of Hurricane Katrina. He asked some of the world's most inventive designers to provide prototypes for resilient homes that could withstand the next big storm. The houses, which his nonprofit foundation, Make It Right, planned to build in a section of the Lower Ninth Ward, would have to be raised above the ground to meet federal flood standards, conserve as much energy as possible, and provide homeowners with an area of refuge. The kicker was that the homes would have to cost $150,000 or less to build. Pitt intended to sell them to displaced residents with subsidies. The program stirred controversy by producing some real curiosities—houses with unusual shapes, bright colors, and ambitious sustainability agendas. Many seemed out of place; they were unlike anything Lower Ninth residents had lost. And eleven years after the hurricane, some residents filed a class-action lawsuit saying their homes were poorly constructed. Nevertheless, the houses are examples of innovative flood design.

Make It Right streetscape. *Photos by Boyce Thompson*

The prototype Float house by Thom Mayne and a team
of UCLA students sits on a 4,600-pound concrete
chassis. Its design proved too expensive to replicate.

The No. 9 House by Kieran Timberlake allows flood-waters to pass underneath, and a trellis, which recalls Italianate details in older New Orleans neighborhoods, moderates solar heat gain.

Billes Partners' cost-efficient design included protected car parking and a usable front porch. Variations on the design, in different color schemes and configurations, help unify the neighborhood fabric.

The 1,000-square-foot Float house, designed by Los Angeles architect Thom Mayne and his team, and students at UCLA, received the most attention. The home sits on a 46,000-pound concrete chassis that includes its mechanical, electrical, plumbing, and green systems. In high water, the chassis works like a raft, rising up to 12 feet on steel guideposts anchored in concrete. Solar panels power the home, a concave roof collects rainwater, and a ground-source heat pump cools and heats the house. The house proved so expensive to build, mostly because of the chassis, that it never went beyond the prototype stage. Make It Right reportedly asked the design team for a less expensive version, but it never happened.

Architects at Kieran Timberlake, Philadelphia, took a more conventional approach to the challenge, raising their No. 9 house permanently aboveground so that floodwaters could pass underneath. They innovatively outfitted the 1,520-square-foot home with a chassis foundation that could accept a variety of structural components, depending on the floor plan buyers wanted. Early versions included a mix of factory-built shells, structural insulated panels (SIPs), and site-built components. Like the Float House, No. 9 produced its own electricity and collected water. Its fanciful trellis, reminiscent of Italianate details in older New Orleans neighborhoods, moderated solar heat gain. The flood-ready design proved cost-efficient to build and was replicated several times.

The neighborhood benefited from a midcourse correction made by Pitt, who reached out to local architects for designs that would look more like they belonged in New Orleans. One home designed by the local firm Billes Partners was reproduced more than seventeen times, partly because it could be constructed cost-efficiently, but also because it included protected car parking and a usable front porch, two things locals said in focus groups that they wanted. The design looks familiar to New Orleans, even as an unusual roof angle gives it a modern character. The repetition of the Billes design, in different color schemes and slightly different configurations, brought cohesion to the neighborhood of 150 homes.

ONLY PASSING THROUGH

Trolley House

Rowayton, Connecticut

Bruce Beinfield

3,400 square feet

It's not a matter of *if* the Trolley house will flood but *when*. Architect Bruce Beinfield's personal residence occupies a delicate spit of land, only 25 feet wide, in the middle of an estuary that rises and falls with sea tides. The "lot," created with rubble fill in 1894, formerly lodged a trolley line that shuttled customers to Roton Park, a long-gone seaside amusement park remembered for its pristine beaches and granite rock outcroppings. The amusement park was decimated by a hurricane in 1938. Only faded photographs and parts of an elevated track bed remain.

Beinfield offers his 75-foot-long home near Norwalk, Connecticut, as a teaching laboratory for resisting the major storms that strike New England with growing frequency. The lesson starts with raising most of the home on concrete piers 15 feet above the ground, 2 feet higher than federal flood regulations require. Where the structure does touch ground, at the entry and garage, flood vents in reinforced concrete walls allow water to pass through. Flood damage typically occurs when outside water, with no place to go, pushes on a wall. Flood vents stabilize hydrostatic pressure on either side of the wall, reducing the potential for damage. Federal guidelines allow enclosed

Bruce Beinfield's home near Norwalk, Connecticut, sits at the edge of an estuary that rises and falls with the sea. It occupies a slice of land that used to support trolley tracks to a seaside amusement park. *Photos © Robert Benson Photography*

spaces below the floodplain as long as they have flood vents and the walls of the enclosed space rise above the flood level.

When storms approach, Beinfield can roll down shutters to cover the home's big openings. Invisible from the exterior, hidden behind bracing, the shutters can sustain category 5 hurricane winds of up to 200 miles per hour. When the shutters are open, as they are on most days, banks of divided-light windows fill the home with sunlight. Concrete floors collect radiant heat to warm the house at night, when the shutters can be closed to prevent heat loss. They are assisted by beefed-up insulation in the exoskeleton. When it's really cold, radiant floor heaters and a high-efficiency heat pump provide backup heat.

Beinfield drew design inspiration from sepia-toned photos of the old amusement park. They showed a series of vibrant, barnlike structures and a diagonally braced wooden roller coaster. Beinfield's home, partly built with salvaged wood, could be confused for an old barn. Bracing on the exterior walls picks up on the trestle of the roller coaster. The interiors pay homage to the industrial heritage of the early twentieth century with a palette of timbers, raw steel, concrete, and copper.

The narrow lot could support only a 12.5-foot-wide street façade. That turned out to be a blessing because it allows passersby to see Farm Creek from the road. Beinfield encountered local environmental opposition to his project when first proposed, even though a

---

A rustic, industrial design pays homage to the area's barnlike structures and old roller coaster. The house sits on concrete piers 15 feet above the ground except at the entry and garage, where flood vents in reinforced concrete walls allow water to pass through.

Hidden, roll-down shutters protect the home from hurricanes.

Steel beams separate five activity zones within the long, narrow home. The zones are unified by a concrete floor, long mechanical runs, and a wall of cabinets.

small cottage already occupied the site. He agreed to move the new house closer to the road and keep it out of the estuary. The waterway and adjacent wildland area is a favorite of birders. Lucky ones can spot oystercatchers, ibis, heron, and many other shorebirds, some endangered.

Inside, steel girders and mechanical runs, rather than applied molding, delineate five carefully conceived living zones. Operable steel windows—9 feet high and 7.5 feet wide—center on each zone. The entry zone, consisting of a foyer and stair hall, was designed to engage guests, encourage exploration, and shed expectations. A more utilitarian service zone, wrapped in fir plywood, is where work gets done. It encompasses the laundry room, powder room, mechanical room, pantry, mudroom, gallery, and a computing station. Concrete flooring, spiral duct work, and a 45-foot cabinet run tie the zones together.

The home was designed to foster an intimate relationship with marsh wildlife. Sliding glass-panel doors in the living room and master bedroom open directly to the estuary. An herb garden window above the kitchen galley sink receives morning sunlight. Other sustainable details include salvaged extinct heart pine used to build open shelving in the dining room. Tall shelves for books and collectibles bring to life a library over the garage; it's an ideal spot to study up on the estuary wildlife.

In the kitchen, unfinished copper and brass surfaces change color with the light.

Robust concrete block, used to form the fireplace walls, challenges conventional building material hierarchies.

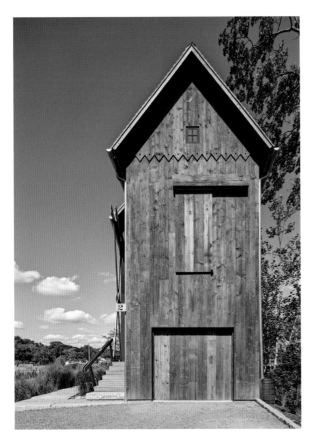

The sun rises through bedroom windows with concealed interior shutters.

A narrow front façade ensures that passersby can still enjoy estuary views.

CREATING A NATURAL WATER BUFFER

It's hard to tell where Farm Creek estuary ends and Beinfield's "yard" begins. The architect planted the grounds around his house with native species to expand habitat opportunities for the birds, reptiles, and mammals that make up the estuary's ecosystem. He had an ulterior motive too. The plants' deep roots help his yard resist the deepening forces of erosion. They also naturally filter out pollutants.

"With climate change and rising sea levels, the use of native, natural grasses makes sense along the shoreline," says Beinfield. "A healthy estuary system populated with native plants has a remarkable ability to absorb the impact of major weather events. Native grasses have adapted over thousands of years to be quite resilient, with deep root systems that anchor the soil around them."

The living shoreline starts with Northwind switchgrass, hardy and salt tolerant. Large swaths of little bluestem and big bluestem grasses that grow up to 6 inches tall form a natural buffer at the site's upland edge. Closer to the house, Beinfield planted spiked gayfeather to attract swarms of butterflies and hummingbirds. He reinforced the shoreline with sausage-like fabric tubes filled with seeded topsoil. Stacked along the bank, they started to green up in days.

Each plant in the living shoreline produces distinctive seeds, nuts, fruits, and shelter to support various species of birds and animals. The ecosystem yields some lively entertainment in the form of coyotes, deer, and sea turtles. All sorts of birds— ducks, egrets, osprey, blue heron, and seagulls—call the estuary home. The architect enjoys watching them go through their daily fish-catching rituals.

© *Robert Benson Photography*

BRACED FOR A BIG ONE

Tsunami House

Camano Island, Washington

Designs Northwest

3,140 square feet

Two hundred years ago, the unspeakable happened on Camano Island—a piece of land broke away and slid into the ocean. The cataclysmic event triggered a tsunami that immersed nearby Hat Island, drowning many of the island's indigenous residents. Though conditions on Camano Island, a vacation spot along the mouth of Washington's Puget Sound, are comparatively calm today, the architects at Designs Northwest decided not to ignore the lessons of history. They designed the 3,140-square-foot Tsunami House along the island's northern shore to take a similar pounding.

The fortifications start with aluminum walls and glass doors on the first level that will break away if a high-velocity wave pummels

Fifty miles from the Tsunami House lies the Cascadia subduction zone, a 680-mile stretch of colliding plates that forms one of the largest active fault lines in North America. *Photos by Lucas Henning*

Glass doors, purposely set in weak frames, would break away in a storm surge, allowing rushing water to flow through the home's bottom chamber and out the opposite side.

the house. "They are actually attached to the concrete with plastic screws rather than stainless steel," explains architect Dan Nelson, whose firm specializes in resilient architecture. Allowing water to flow through the bottom level and out the opposite side reduces the pressure on piers that support the structure's two upper levels. As designed, the house should withstand the impact of crashing waves up to 8 feet.

An earthquake, a more likely event to afflict Camano Island, would also struggle to bring down the house. The pillars support a cast-in-place concrete frame tied to a 30-inch mat slab reinforced with steel rebar. The frame is designed to withstand the shocks and aftershocks of a 7.8-magnitude earthquake. That's the strongest event that an earthquake-resistant building could withstand. "The concept here is that the mat slab foundation and the concrete columns move together if there is an earthquake or if the home is hit by a high-velocity wave," says Nelson. "The system acts as a single structural unit."

Losses within the first-floor flood room would be limited too. Everything on this level has been certified waterproof, and there are no electrical outlets. Most of the space is taken up by outdoor furniture. Radiant heating in the concrete floor warms the space on cool days. Clear-glass overhead doors open to a waterside deck facing north, filling the room with light. On the south side facing the entry courtyard, Nelson specified overhead doors with translucent glass to provide more privacy.

Watertight construction will protect the house from lateral winds of up to 85 miles an hour. The home's steel cladding, metal roofing, and aluminum-framed, tempered-glass windows easily exceed safety requirements for waterfront homes outlined by FEMA and the

A porous deck covers a water filtration system with drains buried in sand. Homes on Camano Island must provide their own septic.

Glass doors in the "flood room" under the house close from overhead, filling in between concrete columns that support the upper levels.

Army Corps of Engineers. An ice and water shield membrane, applied over roof sheathing before the metal roofing goes down, protects the home if its roofing flies off in a storm. If the power goes out, a backup generator plugs into a dedicated receptacle to run key systems.

The remote location required other inspired resiliencies. There's no public sewer service on Camano Island; each home needs its own septic system. Nelson, working within the confines of a shallow lot, hid an aboveground sand filter drain below a pervious sun deck. Three-foot-high architectural concrete walls encase the deck, creating privacy from the street when the flood room's overhead garage doors are open.

The extreme defenses combine with a relaxed floor plan to promote worry-free weekends at the beach. A bent-plate steel staircase rises from the flood room to the main level, where kitchen, living, and dining zones sit in an open plan. A long wall of windows provides panoramic sea views from any spot in the room. Sliding translucent doors in the master bedroom offer a water view as well.

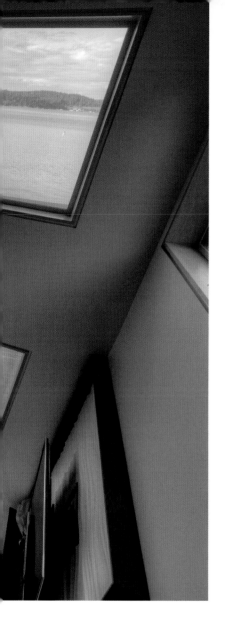

Nelson nurses no illusions about whether the home could survive a tsunami like the one in the Indian Ocean in 2004 that killed about a quarter-million people. There's no such thing as a tsunami-proof home, he says, just as there is no such thing as a hurricane- or tornado-proof home. But most damage, he points out, is done by lesser storms, and a lot of it can be avoided by taking precautions. Raised about 9 feet above sea level, with its lower level designed to give way, the Tsunami House certainly stands a fighting chance.

A wide-open, vaulted floor plan preserves ocean views from public spaces. Large window expanses make it seem like the home is at sea.

The house juxtaposes expansive views with intimate spaces such as this compact cabin bath tucked under the stairs.

Positioning the galley kitchen along a side wall of the shallow home allows the entire width to be used as a great room.

A western red cedar ceiling warms an industrial palette of steel, concrete, and glass. A ship ladder leads to a small hideaway loft.

A decrepit concrete seawall remains from the days before a new home was built on the site.

THE WASH-AND-WEAR HOUSE

Hurricane Katrina not only wiped out entire New Orleans neighborhoods, it also raised serious questions about how to design resilient homes in flood-prone regions. Against that backdrop, one of the nation's leading building scientists, Joe Lstibruek, popularized what he called the Wash-and-Wear House. The idea was to build a home that not only would resist the forces of water and wind but could be hosed off and reoccupied quickly after a storm. The scientist worked closely with Claudette Reichel of Louisiana State University to perfect the concept. "In Louisiana, we flood somewhere once a year," says Reichel. "If you use material that's washable and dryable, you don't have to gut and replace stuff."

Lstibruek and Reichel recommend building the lower levels of a home, if not the entire home, with concrete block. Many builders, of course, would prefer to frame homes with wood—it's less expensive and easier to work with. But when wood gets wet, it takes a long time to dry. And if it stays wet for a long time, it may need to be replaced. The scientists would eliminate as much wood as possible, including wood sheathing used to reinforce walls.

Lstibruek advises installing a layer of extruded polystyrene sheathing (EXPS) inside block or brick siding, separated by an airspace. Then he would cover the sheathing with closed-cell foam insulation, easily obtained in most major housing markets. Research shows that closed-cell foam, in addition to being easy to wash, provides racking resistance. "The foam adds structural capacity to make up for the lack of sheathing," says Reichel, who recommends using only as much foam insulation as required by code.

The next step is to coat the interior with an acrylic latex paint to facilitate the wash, rinse, and dry cycles after a flood. The pair would finish interior walls with gypsum, leaving gaps halfway up the wall and at the top and bottom, and cover them with horizontal wood trim. That way, after a flood, the trim can be removed to pull drywall easily from the wall, allowing the interior to dry out. "The gypsum is a goner anyway," says Lstibruek. That's especially true, he adds,

when black, polluted water enters homes, as it did during Hurricane Harvey in Texas.

"After a flood," Reichel says, "all you have to do is flush the walls with a nonphosphate detergent, do a rinse, use dehumidifiers to dry the walls quickly, and replace the drywall or wainscoting, and you are back in your home. You don't have to wait on materials or contractors to do the work. The problem after a flood is that everyone needs to repair their home at the same time. You wait in line. There's a shortage of materials and qualified contractors."

Lstibruek has many builder followers in Florida, where concrete block construction is the norm due to a beefed-up building code. Their homes were put to the test by a recent storm. "Homes built this way had absolutely no issues after Hurricane Irma," he says. "Naples, Florida, was hit with sustained 140 mph winds. The trees did not fare well, but the new houses laughed it off. A few tiles blew off and almost every window leaked. Interiors dried quickly, though, and Naples was back in shape."

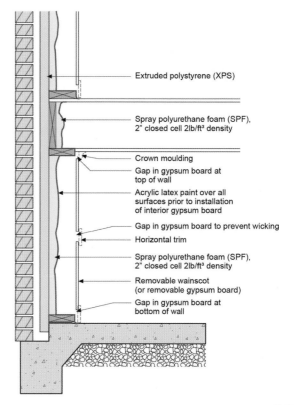

Extruded polystyrene (XPS)

Spray polyurethane foam (SPF), 2" closed cell 2lb/ft³ density

Crown moulding

Gap in gypsum board at top of wall

Acrylic latex paint over all surfaces prior to installation of interior gypsum board

Gap in gypsum board to prevent wicking

Horizontal trim

Spray polyurethane foam (SPF), 2" closed cell 2lb/ft³ density

Removable wainscot (or removable gypsum board)

Gap in gypsum board at bottom of wall

Diagram courtesy of Building Science Corporation

EARTH

MORE THAN 20 STATES HAVE A MODERATE OR HIGH RISK OF DAMAGING EARTHQUAKES.

You think you are standing on solid ground. But with each passing year, storm surges eat away at shorelines, leaving prized oceanside homes clinging to bluffs. Elsewhere, prolonged droughts and wildfires kill hillside vegetation. Then when rains come, the ground gives way and huge slides of mud and debris bury vast tracts of land. Meanwhile, spring rains come early in the mountains, melting snow packs and triggering landslides. Landslides can occur in all fifty states, but mountain regions, including the Appalachians and Ozarks, are most vulnerable.

Homes in some regions have always required protection from geohazards. Swelling clay soils undermine foundations and crack walls in the Southwest. Water-logged, silty soils cause frost heaves in the North that damage incorrectly founded garages and decks. Then there's the spreading danger of deep sinkholes, formed when water dissolves rocks underground. News reports show them gobbling up homes in Florida, Missouri, Texas, and

Photo courtesy of Fougeron Architecture,
Joe Fletcher Photography

Pennsylvania. The biggest geological threat, though, may be earthquakes, which occur in more states than people realize.

Global warming has raised the stakes posed by unstable ground. Landslides, in particular, appear to be growing in frequency and intensity. In the biggest recent slide, heavy rainfall over a period of thirty-five days collapsed portions of an unstable hill in Oso, Washington. The breakdown produced a fast-moving wall of mud and debris that killed forty-three people and destroyed forty-nine structures. When heavy rains melted the local snowpack near Collbran, Colorado, it led to the West Salt Creek landslide, which buried almost 600 acres of land and killed three people. More recently, twenty-one people died from mud-flows in Santa Barbara, Los Angeles, and Ventura Counties that came one month after wildfires deforested nearby hills.

FEMA warns that more than twenty states—not just California, Alaska, and Washington—have a moderate or high risk of damaging earthquakes. Within the past 200 years, major upheavals have occurred in Charleston, South Carolina; and Memphis, Tennessee. The Charleston earthquake destroyed much of the city. Smaller, damaging earthquakes have shaken Los Angeles and Seattle during the last fifty years. A 1964 earthquake in Prince William Sound, Alaska, triggered landslides that destroyed a large portion of Anchorage, taking out an entire subdivision. FEMA provides this sobering guidance: wherever earthquakes happen, they are likely to occur again.

Few homes are built to resist earth tremors. In fact, most building codes outside California, Washington, and Alaska ignore the threat, even though designing a home to resist an earthquake isn't that difficult. Fortunately, model code bodies—their work available on the internet—publish seismic-safety provisions based on the latest engineering technology. The biggest issues are giving buildings lateral support, since earthquakes shake them sideways, and carefully anchoring walls and roof. Even local governments that regularly adopt new provisions in model building codes may exclude seismic provisions because they add expense.

It makes sense for many reasons to consider what lurks below the ground—and around the perimeter of the lot—before you build. Many new homes are built on lots that may have been passed over for good reason. They may be too close to a shoreline that has shifted. Hidden streams may run underneath them. Or dangers may have disappeared from view; perhaps a wetland temporarily dried up or a contaminated building was plowed under. The phrase "buyer beware" was seemingly invented to describe the risk of land transactions, and global warming only magnifies the need for due diligence.

CALLING THE BLUFF

The Fall House

Big Sur, California

Fougeron Architecture

3,800 square feet

A system of pillars anchors the Fall House to rock above a cliff on Big Sur's south coast. *Photos courtesy of Fougeron Architecture, Joe Fletcher Photography*

The residents of Big Sur have grown accustomed to occasional erosion that closes Highway 1, the winding coastal road cut into the face of seaside bluffs. Small landslides happen frequently enough that locals give them clever names—Arleen's Slide honors a popular flagger who was standing on the roadside when part of a hillside gave way. But the citizenry was hardly prepared when in 2017, after five years of drought, heavy rains caused a huge chunk of coastline to fall. Earth from the Mud Creek landslide could have filled 800 Olympic-sized swimming pools. It buried Highway 1 more than 65 feet deep, closing the route for a year.

The Fall House survived unscathed. The home was thoughtfully set back 12 feet from the edge of a cliff that drops 250 feet to the Pacific, even though ocean views may have been better closer to the cliff. Moving it away from the edge protected the cliff's delicate ecosystem, providing at least a hundred years of insurance against erosion. A retaining wall on the uphill portion of the lot protects the house from falling debris. "No one can plan for the intensity of Mother Nature, and some element is luck," says architect Anne Fougeron, who designed the house. "That being said, we were incredibly diligent and meticulous in our siting, foundation, and material choosing."

It's hard to imagine this home tumbling into the sea. It rests on steel piers driven 10 to 30 feet into stable bedrock. The rock-solid

cantilevered room closest to the cliff lifts its head like a slug ready to strike. Visitors enter at the top of the upper volume. As they descend through the house, living spaces unfold from the most public to the most private. Subtle changes in floor levels and ceiling planes mark activity zones within an open living, dining, and kitchen space. An all-glass library, the most dynamic room in the house, appears suspended over the ocean. In the lower-level bedroom suite, floor-to-ceiling windows look out on rolling waves and a setting sun.

Unlike the monolithic banana slug, two facades define an upper and lower volume connected by the glass library. The standing-seam copper roof wraps down to clad the south wall, and overhangs shelter the windows and front door from the sun and ocean winds. On the shadier north façade, clear-glass expanses open the house to sea views. A one-story concrete bunker, perpendicular to the house, contains a ground-floor bedroom, building services, and a green roof. It acts like an enormous anchor tying the house to the ground.

The omnipresent threat of fire guided the selection of exterior materials—no surprise, given that woods surround the house and droughts beset the region. "It was of tantamount importance that all the exterior materials be fire resistant, even the windows," says Fougeron. "In fires, glass tends to explode and let fire into the house. We used a tempered, laminated glass that cannot shatter. On the inside, the house is equipped with more than two dozen sprinklers. I brought in fire extinguishers myself," she says.

The home uses thermal mass and solar orientation to its advantage and to reduce dependence on fossil fuels. The main body acts as a shield, protecting outdoor space on the south side from potent northwest winds. Windows on the south side were kept to a minimum and outfitted with an automatic shading system. Most daylight reaches the interior indirectly from the glass-walled north side.

foundation insulates the house from seismic forces as well as erosion. Strapping connects the home's steel frame to its foundation, plywood shear walls, and copper roof. The resulting moment frame works as a single unit if the earth shakes, resisting both vertical and lateral forces. Most building codes protect homes only from vertical forces. But earthquakes shake a building side to side. "Every structural element had to be earthquake prepared," says Fougeron.

She compares the house's long, thin form and the way it hugs the slope to banana slugs native to the region's seaside forests. Two rectangular boxes with a slanting roofline, the structure zigzags its way down the slope. A

The house zigzags down a slope, hugging the ground like a banana slug.

A retaining wall outlines a sunken porch and protects it from mudslides.

Sustainably harvested wood trim combines with
low-VOC paints and stains and formaldehyde-free
denim insulation to produce breathe-easy interiors.

Automatic skylights and windows in the transparent library work with an exhaust grill on the upper level to naturally ventilate the house.

A patio off the kitchen provides killer ocean views.

The structure's drop in elevation, coupled with open connections between the two levels, allows it to be cooled with stacked ventilation. Windows open automatically on the lowest level to accept sea breezes, which are pulled up through the house by an exhaust transfer grille at the highest elevation. Most of the mechanical heating comes from radiant heaters in the French limestone floors. They eliminate duct work and require less energy to operate than traditional forced-air systems.

A stream on the property provides fresh water. Water consumption is minimized with low-flow toilets, and gray water from showers and faucets gets recycled for other uses around the house. Black water from toilets is routed through the municipal sewer system. Drought-resistant and native vegetation reduces soil erosion and provides new habitats for local wildlife. Viewed from above, a vegetated roof blends the building into its landscape even as it insulates the living space below.

Windows on the sparsely fenestrated south side close automatically when the sun is too hot. Workers wore repelling gear to install the roof glazing.

Drawing courtesy of Fougeron Architecture

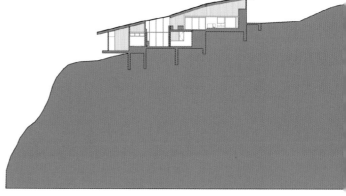

 0   32'   SITE PLAN & SECTION

HOW LATERAL FORCES AFFECT A HOME

Most houses are designed and built to resist vertical forces—the weight of snow on the roof, the weight of appliances and furniture in the house, and the building itself. But earthquakes and high winds also exert lateral forces parallel to the ground that can come from any direction. A structural engineer may have to be called in for guidance.

The basic idea is to transfer vertical and lateral loads through the building to the ground. Loads accumulate as they are routed through key connections—straps that tie roofs to walls, anchors that bolt walls to foundations. Headers over windows and doors, for example, transfer loads to studs on the side of the opening. Failed or missed structural connections reroute loads through components such as flimsy wall sheathing that aren't able to handle them. Buildings may fail as a result.

The path for vertical loads is pretty straightforward—from the roof or floor, through supporting walls, through the floors below, to the foundation, and to the ground. Lateral loads move from the roof or floor into the walls parallel to the force, then to the foundation and into the ground. To resist them requires the use of shear walls, with additional base anchor bolts, hold-down anchors, and tighter nailing. Shear walls are typically built with plywood or OSB (oriented strand board) covered with rigid or spray foam insulation and braced with drywall.

Diagrams courtesy of APA, the Engineered Wood Association

LATERAL LOAD PATH

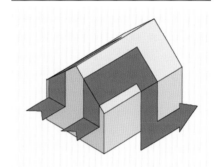

VERTICAL LOAD PATH

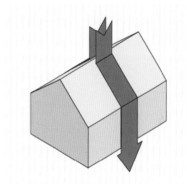

SEISMIC FORCES ACTING ON MASS

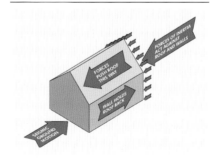

MUDSLIDE SLIM

Saratoga Hill House

Camano Island, Washington

Designs Northwest Architects

1,926 square feet

Even the untrained eye can see the hillside scars left by mud and rocks that periodically slide down the cliff behind the Saratoga Hill House. When the owners of a small family cabin on the site decided they wanted a bigger house, geological engineers were called in to do a feasibility analysis. They determined the spot was unsafe for conventional building techniques and recommended building a 20-foot-tall concrete retaining wall behind the house to catch falling debris.

That would be easier said than done. The lot is located along a remote, environmentally restricted beach without road access on the west side of Camano Island on Puget Sound. "It would have been impossible to get a concrete truck to the site," says Dan Nelson of Designs Northwest Architects. "It would have sunk into the sand." Nelson decided to take a completely different tack: elevate the structure out of harm's way. He developed plans to set thirteen 9-foot-high steel columns into concrete footings. The house's main living portions would be suspended over a drain field. The building department and geotechnical firm approved the approach.

But even that tactic created challenges. Workers had to mix concrete for the footings in a public parking lot down the beach, then drive forklifts with wet concrete batches along a path

The home's remote location beneath a large cliff on a protected seashore made traditional building techniques unfeasible. *Photos by Lucas Henning*

Water, rocks, and soil that flow down the cliff are channeled under the main portion of a house safely suspended on steel columns.

A steel moment frame ties the structural elements together so that they move as one during an earthquake.

adjacent to the beach bulkhead. They poured the footings with a custom chute. There were scheduling constraints too. Building materials could be taken to the site only at certain times of the year—when smelt weren't breeding along the shore. Their eggs are a favorite of protected wild salmon. A biologist monitored the site to make sure the smelt weren't disturbed.

The complicated foundation work protects the house not only from falling debris, but also rising water and storm surges. The pier foundation allows mudslides and raging waters to pass under the house. They can move unfettered under the northern end of the house, which is cantilevered over a fern garden. The ground level is used primarily to store canoes, kayaks, beach umbrellas, and other items that the owners can afford to have wash away.

Nelson linked the concrete footings to provide lateral support during earthquakes; they occur regularly on and around the island, though most can't be felt. He tied the structural elements together to form a moment frame. The steel columns, foundation, shear panels, and

roof sheathing move together and stay rigid when tremors shake the ground. The US Geological Survey (USGS) estimates that in the next fifty years there's a 78.6 percent of a major earthquake on Camano Island. The island has had 483 minor quakes since 1931.

The owners wanted to make sure they could ride out strong winds and rain too. Metal siding, attached as a rainscreen system, repels wind-driven rain. If water manages to get behind the cladding, air space between the siding and a waterproof membrane attached to wall sheathing drains it away. Another membrane under the metal roof guards against ice dams that occur when water from melting snow refreezes along roof overhangs. It can back up under shingles, weaken underlayment, and lead to leaks. A backup generator powers lights and receptacles when utility power isn't available.

Unlike the old cabin, the new 1,926-square-foot house provides enough space for visits

---

A combined living room and kitchen feature ocean views uninterrupted by the staircase.

Walls of windows disappear into hidden frames. Steel beams and concrete floors give the home industrial character.

from children and grandchildren. Concrete stairs lead from the ground level to the main living areas. Floor-to-ceiling glass on the second and third floors provides uninterrupted views of gray and killer whales in the Saratoga Passage. A terraced roof deck on the third floor, used primarily by guests, provides an even better vantage. The home's east side, facing the steep slope, has more opaque walls with selected views of hillside vegetation.

Harmony with the natural environment drives the design of the best homes built each year. In most cases, that's a simple matter of trying to take advantage of great views, cool breezes, and natural topography. The threats of moving earth, driving rain, and high winds magnified the challenge on the Saratoga House. It almost betrays the complicated nature of the project when Nelson says, "The design is a direct response to its site."

Steel columns set in concrete suspend the house, protecting it from mudflows and storm surges.

A terraced roof deck, ideal for whale watching, looks out to the Saratoga Passage.

Metal roofing and siding join with water-resistant windows and doors to defend against wind-driven rain.

ROOT OF THE MATTER

South 5th Street

Austin, Texas

Alterstudio

2,990 square feet

Who knows what surprises lurk below the ground of an infill lot? Engineers called in to bore earth samples may find hidden complications such as shifting sandy soils, construction backfill, or underground springs. Poor soil can wreak havoc on a traditional foundation and even cause homes to slide down a hill. Root systems of protected trees can cause other complications. A thorough geologic investigation may provide a pretty clear picture of why the lot sits empty.

The owners of the South 5th Street project held their breath when soil engineers drilled four holes in their steep, empty lot in the heart of Austin's eclectic Bouldin District. The engineers sought to determine whether the ground was likely to settle or heave, information that would establish what kind of foundation the home would require. Sure enough, the dig revealed deeply deposited and poorly compacted fill material in spots, along with silty clay and layers of stable limestone at varying depths. They also found that the roots of a protected twenty-five-year-old Durand oak "took up most of the 50-foot-wide lot," says architect Kevin Alter.

Alter designed a home with a delicate footprint to work around the constraints. Steel columns suspend the living room and protect the home by allowing any sliding earth to flow under the house. The Durand oak became the centerpiece of an entry courtyard. A second protected tree, a live oak, occupies an interior courtyard that serves as a focal point for key rooms. "Slipping the house in between these two trees, and within the zoning tent, required quite a bit of gymnastics," says Alter. The architect was rewarded with a national award from the American Institute of Architects.

The owners' desire for a basement—never an easy proposition in southwestern states with potentially unstable soils—further complicated matters. The soil report found that part of the basement would have to rest on deep fill material that could move and crack a traditional foundation. Pier shafts had to be drilled into limestone 18 feet below the ground for support. Fortunately, the ground was strong enough in other spots to accommodate a less expensive, soil-supported floor slab.

The house deftly negotiates zoning and envelope requirements to slip nonchalantly into the neighborhood. A monolithic concrete street façade belies the openness of the interiors. Visitors arrive to a constricted entryway that gives no clue to the views beyond. Around the corner, a long hallway culminates in a distant view of trees through floor-to-ceiling glass. Moving through the house, visitors pass a floating stairwell and a glass-lined interior courtyard that houses the live oak. The hall

Unstable soil on a steeply sloping lot required a reinforced foundation for this Austin house. *Photos by Casey Dunn*

Piers buried deep into bedrock protect the house from a landslide. The living room appears to hang within a tree canopy.

A protected oak that occupies the glass-walled
courtyard serves as a focal point for interior views.

Patio doors in the rear open to ventilate the house. Sunken frames make the windows disappear.

ends in a glassy living room with views across the valley. "The setting up of expectations, and unexpected discoveries along the way, were central to our design," Alter says.

So was a passive ventilation strategy in the event storms lead to power outages. The house was sited to take advantage of prevailing breezes from the valley below. Screened ventilator doors in the back draw cool air through open spaces on the first floor. Air rises through the open internal stairwell and exits through second-floor windows. There isn't much need for backup heat if power goes out during the winter. "Going without air conditioning is a much-bigger concern than going without heat in this climate," Alter says.

Low-emissivity glass in most windows and patio doors helps prevent the house from overheating in the summer. "In the living room corner where glass meets glass, we used laminated glass rather than insulated glass," Alter says. "This allows us to turn the corner without anything blocking the transparency, and the effect is quite remarkable. In our

Alter's floor plan intentionally alternates between intimate spaces and expansive views.

climate we can afford to lose the insulation. We generally don't suffer from condensation or other problems here."

The glass-walled internal courtyards create the impression that the home was built with light cubes. Its airiness is balanced by textured, tactile surfaces—concrete, mill-finished steel, finely detailed millwork, and raw stucco. While the extensive use of floor-to-ceiling glass made privacy a big concern, a perforated, corrugated wall screens the view of neighbors to the south, and a 4-inch-wide gabion wall conceals the entry courtyard from the street.

The family-friendly floor plan provides opportunities to spend high-quality time both together and alone. On the first floor are a kitchen/dining area, media room, and guest bedroom. Two more bedrooms are upstairs, including a master suite perched above the trees with views of Lake Austin. A second, more intimate living area in the basement includes a family room, gym, and deck, and patio doors connect it directly to the backyard. Because of the sloped yard, the basement rooms still look out into the tree canopy, yet they are firmly rooted in the earth.

The family can watch comings and goings in the eclectic neighborhood from a bedroom suspended over parking.

Kitchen, dining, and living spaces are set up along the back of the family-oriented house, with a second family area in the walkout basement.

RESISTING THE FLOW

Teaberry

Tiburon, California

Cary Bernstein Architect

1,100 square feet

Building a new bedroom wing on a flat side yard looked like an easy proposition—until geologists examined the soil. *Photos by Cesar Rubio, courtesy of Cary Bernstein Architect*

The business of adding a new master bedroom wing to this house, on a sloped hillside overlooking northern San Francisco Bay, appeared easy enough. A level side yard looked like the ideal location. The owners could imagine waking to the sound of gulls moving across the water, watching colorful yachts pass from a private deck, and sharing a spacious new bathroom removed from the bustle of the main house. Then the geotechnical report came in.

It showed that the side yard—in fact the entire terrace on which the house sits—rested on loose fill created by excavating the slope above the house. Moreover, the cut had exposed silty cobble deposits that had washed or

A new concrete retaining wall protects the home and addition against rock slides.

slid down the lot, creating a "prominent landscape scar" of up to 60 feet. Portions of the slope adjacent to the wound showed "older earthflows." The forces of moving earth and water had taken their toll on the house, which sits on raised wood joists. The foundation had cracked on one side. Deck supports on the downslope side had moved.

The engineers recommended building the addition on piers driven deep into the ground. They also advocated constructing a 50-foot-long retaining wall to protect both the existing home and addition from debris tumbling down the hill. The recommendations added considerable expense and complication to what the owners thought would be a simple project. "The report was a surprise," says architect Cary Bernstein, adding that her clients at first resisted the added expense. "But they followed our direction and are now really happy that they have the wall for both aesthetic and functional reasons."

The retaining wall, built with board-formed concrete, became part of a comprehensive erosion plan that includes bioretention planters, swales, and extensive site drainage. Bernstein likes the way the wall's bulk contrasts with the lightness of the addition, which appears to float above the ground because of its concrete platform. Using concrete to form both the retaining wall and the plinth connects the landscape and the house as one idea, she says.

Other game-changers had occurred since the original home was built. California now requires new homes and additions to be protected from wildfires and earthquakes. To strengthen the addition's lateral support, Bernstein drew a platform of concrete grade beams that lie on top of the piers. Walls went on top of the grade beams, and then the assembly was tied together. "The fundamentals of earthquake resilience are building on good soils, which we didn't have; embedment in bedrock, which, in this case, is the role of the

California's wildfire code prohibited highly flammable vegetation near the house.

An orange panel marks the junction between old and new. The entryway frames a tantalizing view of San Francisco Bay.

piers; and then a structural design—wood, steel, or concrete—that can take the lateral forces, which may be similar to wind loads in other places," she says.

Wildfire code requires the use of nonflammable or fire-resistant materials on and around the house. This resulted in the use of concrete around the perimeter, rock gardens under windows, and heavy timber landscape stairs. When wood is used on the exterior, per

California's code, it needs to be at least 2 inches thick or backed with a layer of gypsum. A light commercial–grade sprinkler system was installed as additional fire protection.

The addition, which nearly doubled the house's square footage, is clad in small-scale cedar siding that quietly departs from the wide planks on the original structure. Bernstein unified the new and old portions through overhangs, dark massing, and the concrete retaining wall, while expressive orange panels mark their junction. With the new wing perched 2 feet above the grade of the existing house, landscaping directs water under the bridge and out to the bay side. A concrete mechanical room under the bath anchors the building to the slope, and the master bedroom cantilevers over its foundation, creating a shadowed separation.

The addition's voluminous interior breaks with the older building's small rooms and openings. A bank of multislide doors and windows—composed with clear, translucent, or mirrored glass—fill the addition with daylight. The new rooms mix strong horizontal lines—created by 16-foot vanities and the multislide doors—with vertical counterpoints such as a limestone-clad fireplace. In the bathroom, subtle textures—linen-impressed porcelain and ceramic tile with a reflective glaze—underscore the minimalist presentation.

The addition makes use of a host of green materials—engineered framing lumber, locally

made cabinets and tiles, LED lighting, composite counters, water-based stains and sealers, and low-flow plumbing and fixtures. Energy Star–rated fans turn on automatically when bathroom humidity gets too high, and a 95 percent efficient gas furnace and on-demand hot water conserve resources.

With its handsome retaining wall and accompanying drainage system, the Teaberry house is an example of how well-designed resiliency components can strengthen the home's overall aesthetic.

Patio doors in the master suite provide views of millions of waterfowl that frequent San Francisco Bay, including endangered species such as the California least tern and Ridgway's rail.

A system of piers dug deep into the ground support an addition that sits on fill material. *Diagram by Cary Bernstein Architect*

TEABERRY SECTION - 06.28.18

FIRE, LIKE HIGH WINDS, SEEKS OUT THE WEAKEST LINK IN A HOME'S EXTERIOR.

FIRE

Hotter, drier conditions brought on by a warming climate have doubled the area of the United States affected by forest fires in the last thirty years. The increase, 16,000 square miles, is equal in size to the country of Denmark, according to a paper published in the *Proceedings of the National Academy of Sciences*. A warmer atmosphere creates tinder-dry conditions by sucking water out of live and decaying vegetation and the soil. The conservation practice of putting out fires instead of letting them clear out underbrush contributes to the problem.

It doesn't help that more humans are moving into or near forested areas. Human actions cause more than eight in ten wildfires in western forests. A third stem from campfires, including the Wallow wildfire, the largest in Arizona history. Humans started the Dollar Ridge fire in Utah, which burned more than

Wyoming residence. *Photo by David Agnello*

65,000 acres and upward of seventy homes. A firecracker thrown by a teenager into a parched canyon resulted in a massive wildfire that burned 49,000 acres in Oregon's Columbia River gorge. An illegal burning of paperback books started a fire that scorched 696 acres of land outside Jacksonville, Florida.

Snapped and sparking power lines—a byproduct of residential development—may have been the source of the immense fire that consumed Northern California's wine country in 2017. Twenty-one major wind-driven blazes burned an area equal in size to the state of Indiana, destroying an estimated 8,900 structures and killing forty-four people. One of them, the Tubbs fire, leaped into urban areas that state fire experts believed were safe. Startling news images of decimated Santa Rosa subdivisions drove home the fact that few dwellings can survive the immense force of wildfire burning out of control.

California is one of several governmental bodies that incorporate wildfire safeguards into building codes. The codes promote the use of fire-resistant materials on home exteriors. Concrete walls, metal roofs, and tempered glass give a house a fighting chance against encroaching fire. When wood is used on the exterior, it needs to be thick or backed by gypsum. The codes also dictate fire-safe methods for designing eaves, porches, and fascia, since fire may linger there before working its way inside. Fire, like high winds, seeks out the weakest link in a home's exterior. It breaks through unprotected windows or garage doors. Flying embers find their way inside through a vent or other unprotected opening in the walls or roof.

Because less than 1 percent of western forests burn each year, there's no telling where the next one will occur. Protecting a home requires diligence. Brush needs to be routinely cleared around the yard. Trees must be trimmed so that branches don't touch the house. Woodpiles should be kept 30 feet from the house, even if it makes for a cold walk in the winter. And homeowners need to maintain a clear path to the house for firefighters; it helps if they can draw water from a pool or some other source in the yard. Many of these best practices make sense for people living throughout the country to consider.

OUT OF HARM'S WAY

Wyoming Residence

Jackson Hole, Wyoming

Abramson Teiger Architects

7,000 square feet

Metal siding, roofing, and eaves provide the best of
two worlds—fire resistance and low maintenance.
Photos by David Agnello

Don't be fooled by this home's bucolic setting—a gently sloping meadow outside Jackson Hole, Wyoming. Wildfire is a major threat here. Eight major fires were reported in the Teton Fire District in one year alone. The Cliff Creek fire, a wake-up call for locals, burned 34,000 acres southeast of Jackson Hole, closing the main road to the city. In response to the growing threat, the city adopted a version of the Wildland Urban Interface Code to protect buildings in the path of danger.

Nevertheless, fire safety wasn't top of mind when out-of-towners approached Abramson Teiger Architects about building on their lot. The family's chief instruction: design a vacation home that would require little maintenance, consume scant energy, and improve with age. Those requests, it turns out, dovetailed nicely with fire-safety requirements. Corten steel siding, installed with panels slightly offset to create visual interest, not only resists fire but looks better with age. The same goes for the concrete walls. Angled zinc roofs and eaves that will last decades with minimal care encourage fire to pass over the house rather than linger.

Some of the energy-efficient features add fire resistance as well. Insulating the attic with closed-cell foam to keep it cool eliminated the need for vents, which give fire a path into a house. Triple-glazed, argon-filled, tempered-glass windows discourage radiant-heat buildup should fire reach the house. And the exterior steel rainscreen minimizes thermal bridging while creating a capillary break between the siding and frame.

One place where special fire precautions had to be taken was the crawl space under an elevated wing. The section rests on an engineered wood frame, covered on the underside with two layers of drywall. The assembly should resist fire for at least an hour, theoretically giving firefighters enough time to do their work. If fire starts inside, a sprinkler system—less expensive to install in a new home than an existing one—will automatically douse flames. It even notifies the fire department if fire breaks out when no one's around.

The local fire code also influenced the hardscape and landscape around the house. Its long, inviting driveway had to be big enough for a fire truck to turn around in, and include a turnout so that one truck could pass another. Other than the driveway and a garage recessed into the landscape, construction did little to

Fire-safety regulations required a driveway big enough for fire trucks to pass and a protected crawl space under one wing.

disturb the land. The lot's natural grade was maintained, and the elevated wing, suspended on concrete columns, required minimal foundation work.

The home's low profile—hidden from view looking down the meadow and up from the valley floor—was no accident. Situated on a 1,000-foot butte, the house by regulation had to avoid "skylining." Its shape, when viewed from the valley below, couldn't exceed the profile of the natural topography. The architects drew a low, modest profile facing the

valley, with a roofline that pleasantly mimics the hill's slope. Thanks to piers and a raised deck, the structure almost appears to float above the landscape. On the street side, dynamic overhangs join the suspended wing to make a strong architectural impression.

The grass roof raised major concerns about snow loads. The architects initially thought

A wood-paneled ceiling warms a palette of steel, concrete, and glass.

they might have to support the roof with a concrete frame. But the structural engineer designed a less expensive wood frame that will handle up to 18 inches of snow, or 5 inches of snow saturated with water, and Perlite helped lighten the soil, which is at least 12 inches deep and will resist fire. The roof assembly survived record snowfall in 2017 that caused avalanches and downed utility lines.

The house's ridgeline location, coupled with its overhanging roofline, raised major concerns about roof uplift during high winds: the front elevation features a 6-foot overhang and a cantilever that spans in two directions. Engineers beefed up structural connections in the cantilever, paying particular attention to its vulnerable corner. The house is also engineered to withstand extreme temperature variations—mountain temperatures during summer months can to shift by up to 80 degrees from day to night. A thermal break between the interior and exterior concrete walls—created with 2 inches of rigid insulation—resists outside temperature variations.

Interiors focus on capturing the mountain and valley views in this spectacular location. Bedrooms are arranged along the wall facing the valley. Built-in seating in the main living area—encompassing living, kitchen, and

Triple-glazed, low-e windows protect the interior from extreme radiant heat, and sensitive art from direct sunlight.

Nearby recreational opportunities dictated a different kind of mudroom with storage for tall skiis, benches for putting on boots, and built-in ski-boot warmers.

Relaxed interiors feature tricolored kitchen cabinets, a built-in island sitting nook, and low-profile furniture that won't interfere with mountain views.

dining spaces—brings the volume down to an intimate scale. Wood ceilings, slightly detached from the walls, warm the concrete and stone finishes. Fire resistant and richly patinaed, the home's materials harmonize with the rugged landscape, giving it a strong sense of place—and safety.

Two inches of rigid insulation provide a thermal break between interior and exterior concrete wall surfaces.

WILDLAND URBAN INTERFACE CODE

Jackson Hole is one of many jurisdictions that have adopted versions of the model Wildland Urban Interface Code published by the International Code Council. Fire safety in building codes used to focus primarily on fires started internally from a burning cigarette or short circuit.

As development pushes into former wildlands, additional protections are needed. Driven by strong winds, wildfires can reach peak temperatures within seconds, especially in arid conditions. Initial attacks, though they can be brief, may be followed by spot fires started on and within a home by wind-driven flames and embers.

The Wildland Code attempts to comprehensively limit fire risk. It recommends where to build on a lot—away from slopes, if possible, since fires love to move upland. It prescribes methods to ensure that firefighters have access to a property. And it provides detailed guidance on how to design and build a house that will resist wildfire. Local code provisions can vary from the national code, depending on which version is adopted.

The most recent code prescribes varying levels of fire safety. For the highest level of ignition resistance (preferred by FEMA for areas susceptible to wildfire), it recommends using exterior materials tested to resist fire for up to an hour. That means using what's called a class A roof assembly. Metal roofing, because it's noncombustible, automatically meets that criterion, though because metal transfers heat, FEMA recommends installing fire-resistant battens underneath. Asphalt shingles typically need a gypsum underlayment to qualify. When there's space

between roof decking and covering, like you often see on a tile roof, the model code calls for fire-stopping at the end of the eaves.

Eaves and soffits also need to resist fire for an hour or more. Wood used in these applications must be either 2 inches thick or treated with a fire-retardant chemical. The code approves exterior walls made of noncombustible material such as metal or concrete, along with heavy timbers or logs. Natural wood siding must be backed by fire retardant–treated wood on the exterior side. The code also specifies that siding must run from the top of the foundation to the underside of the roof sheathing to eliminate opportunities for fire to enter the house.

All underfloor areas need to be enclosed to the ground with exterior walls unless they are built with one-hour fire-rated material. Exterior windows, doors, and skylights need to be made with tempered glass, multilayered glazed panels, or glass block or have a fire protection rating of not less than twenty minutes. Wood exterior doors must be made with a solid core 1¾ inches thick or have a fire protection rating of at least twenty minutes.

Vents, an easy entry point for wildfires, are given special attention in the code. The openings can't exceed 144 square inches and must be covered with noncombustible, corrosion-resistant mesh. Attic vents, a particularly big vulnerability, can't be located in soffits, eave overhangs, or between rafters at eaves. Gable end and dormer vents must be at least 10 feet from the property line, and underfloor ventilation openings need to be as close to grade as is practical.

AFTER THE TEA PARTY FIRE

Zen Hacienda House

Santa Barbara, California

DMHA Architecture

2,900 square feet

Stucco wraps the siding, eaves, and facia in a continuous layer, preventing gaps where fire might enter the house. *Photos by Jim Bartsch*

Mike and Diana Wilson, longtime Santa Barbara residents, owned one home that narrowly survived the Sycamore Canyon fire of the early 1970s. When the Tea Party fire ravaged the canyon many years later, they weren't as lucky. The couple returned to their wood-frame home, after evacuating the day before, to find it reduced to flickering embers. "As I came up through the orchard below us, I could see dancing firelight," remembers Mike. "It was clear pretty quickly that we didn't have a house."

The Wilsons thought long and hard about rebuilding in the fire-prone foothills of Santa Barbara, even though they had lived there for forty years. Diana remembers, "I sat and thought to myself, how comfortable are you going to be when the wind blows at night? It's one thing to think it might actually happen, but once you've experienced it, you go, okay, am I nuts?" The Wilsons ultimately decided to do their best to build a "fireproof" house, even though there would be "some nervous nights" when the winds blew.

The couple turned to architect Michael Holliday of DMHA, who himself had lost a home to fire, with clear directions: no combustible materials on the outside (copious light-gauge wood on the exterior of the previous

A sandstone patio, metal trellises, and nonflammable patio furniture may stop fire from reaching house.

house had tempted fate). Holliday selected a palette of fire-resistant building materials—stucco siding, metal roofing and fascia, and cold-rolled steel trellises. The modern materials combine with a familiar ranch form to give the home transitional character.

Because buildings are only as fire-safe as their weakest element, Holliday devoted attention to places where fire is most likely to enter. The advantage of stucco siding is that its uniformity leaves no gaps for fire to penetrate. Stucco continues from the walls through the eaves and to their ends, providing an unbroken line of defense. Builder Gene Vernon paid extra attention to the roof. Roofs are the most vulnerable to fire because of their horizontal orientation and size. "You could have everything figured out but leave one combustible access point and lose your whole house," Holliday says.

The fire-safety precautions complemented the home's energy-conservation agenda. Double-pane, tempered-glass windows, a big improvement over the single-pane windows in the house that burned, protect the interior from the heat of a fire even as they reduce heat loss from inside. Radiant heat from a fire can shatter single-pane windows in five minutes. A low-e coating on the window's interior surface further reduces heat transfer. Insulating the attic with closed-cell foam eliminated the need for attic vents.

Holliday was aided by local design and landscaping guidelines published in the wake of the fire. They emphasize the need to create a defensible space around the house. The line of defense starts with the material used to build porches, decking, and trellises—Holliday specified concrete, stone, and metal instead of wood. The perimeter close to the house was

Unlike its predecessor, which burned down, the new house makes the most of canyon and ocean views.

kept free of high-growth vegetation—and wood furniture—that could catch fire from flying embers and spread to the house.

The design carefully balances the needs of resiliency and livability. Unlike the house that burned, whose floor plan looked inward, the primary living areas enjoy canyon views. Large banks of windows heat the home with sunlight during colder months. Carefully positioned overhangs shade interiors from direct sunlight during summer, when the sun is high in the sky. The master bedroom was positioned to capture distant ocean views.

Holliday used fire-resistant materials for the interiors too—smooth concrete floors and a stone fireplace. They work with a creative interior-lighting scheme and suspended-ceiling accents to create a fresh, modern feel. The use of wood was limited to renewable bamboo kitchen cabinets, stained window and door casements, and molding. The metal roof, set at rakish angles, creates exciting interior volumes.

The Wilsons refer to their home as the Zen Hacienda House because of the way it relates to the natural environment. "The large upper windows allow us to look up into the trees from the master bedroom and living room," says Wilson. "The blue-green polished concrete floor is meant to have a watery feel. The sandstone treatment on the patios makes them feel like a sandy beach. The house is also set on the lot in a way to maximize privacy and views. It's pretty peaceful up here."

A 3.5 kW photovoltaic system, installed after the house was built, provides more electricity than the family needs in most months, running the meter backward. The Wilsons pay only $300 a year for electricity. A backup generator to power essentials—a fridge, a few outlets, and some lighting—during a winter outage is on the family wish list. "Our current approach to losing power is lanterns and fires in the fireplaces," Wilson says.

The need for a generator was reinforced by a recent debris flow that knocked out power briefly and public water for several days. "We were very fortunate on the power side—we had almost no downtime," Wilson says. "But we did lose water for a few days. We filled a couple 5-gallon jugs at my daughter's house that we used for dishes and toilet flushing. It did, however, get us motivated. I put together a much more complete 'earthquake kit.' We installed shelving in our mechanical room and stocked it with four to five days of food, water, and fuel." Just one more line of defense against nature's wrath.

Dining, cooking, and living spaces flow together in an
open plan united by windows and flooring.

CREATING A DEFENSIBLE PERIMETER

The Wilsons followed guidelines published by the City of Santa Barbara and FEMA to create three zones of "defensible space" around their house. In the first zone, closest to the house, the guidelines recommend eliminating flammable vegetation, firewood, combustible furniture, and dimensioned lumber decking. Vines must be prevented from climbing the house, and tree branches must be trimmed away from vents. The instructions also caution against planting trees high in oil content—pine, eucalyptus, and olive—close to the house.

In zone 2, sparse plantings are allowed—individual and well-spaced clumps of trees and shrubs, or a few islands of vegetation surrounded by noncombustible materials. The guidelines suggest using hardscaping—patios, gravel paths, and driveways—to create fire breaks throughout the yard. They permit more vegetation in zone 3, as long as a 20-foot buffer is maintained between plant groups so fire doesn't have a straight path to the house.

The Wilsons irrigate the yard, another FEMA recommendation. They regularly prune trees and recycle dead and dying branches. They pick up vegetation under trees to prevent a ground fire from crowning into trees. They remove litter from roofs and gutters. Strong sundowner winds provide plenty of motivation to keep the yard clear. "Seventy-mile-per-hour gusts are not uncommon," Wilson says. "When fires occur up here during a sundowner event, they are extremely difficult to fight. They happen so quickly that only local fire teams are available. But when winds really kick up, there's not a lot they can do. Your home's best chance of survival is a good fire-resistant exterior and a 'light fuel load' directly upwind."

Although fire can approach from any direction, the most dangerous is when it climbs a hill, consuming fuel along its path. The Wilsons' home is in that position. A wildlands fire expert visits periodically to provide maintenance advice. "We'll use his guidance to direct our tree service in the next few months," Wilson says. "We love the shade that our trees provide, but up here it's critical that their canopies be kept light and clear of dead branches. We do this once a year, before the onset of fire season." Here are other recommendations for creating a defensible perimeter:

• If possible, site your house away from the top of slopes, since upslope-burning fires are the most dangerous.

• Remove woody chaparral around the house but keep large native trees and shrubs because their roots anchor hillsides.

• Work with neighbors to regularly clear the neighborhood of loose vegetation.

• Use nonflammable decking material—brick, tile, or concrete is the safest.

• To assist firefighters, make your pool drainable to an accessible hydrant or pump house or hose.

• Keep a well-maintained pump (diesel, natural gas, or propane) of at least 100-gallon-per-minute capacity with a standard 1½-inch threaded pipe.

• Buy a plastic- or cotton-jacket fire hose (and nozzle) long enough to reach the far side of the house.

• Enclose exterior decks with a nonflammable solid skirt of concrete block, stucco, or cementitious sheeting.

• For fencing, use nonflammable masonry, wrought iron, or chain link.

• Construct arbors or trellises with metal tubing or oversized lumber (4x4s or larger) that takes longer to burn.

Zen Hacienda House. *Photo by Jim Bartsch*

STRAW-BALE SURVIVOR

Rosenberg-Zuckerman Residence

Sonoma, California

Arkin Tilt Architects

1,800 square feet

The Rosenberg-Zuckerman straw-bale house, rimmed by volcanic rock outcroppings, suffered little damage from fires that ravaged Sonoma and Napa Counties. *Photos © EdwardCaldwell.com, except where noted*

David Zuckerman feared the worst as he drove through the charred foothills of Mt. Veeder, anxious to learn whether the house he and Elsa Rosenberg had recently built had survived. News reports put their residence directly in the path of the Norrobom fire, one of twenty-one major conflagrations in Northern California brought on in 2017 by wicked Diablo winds and bone-dry conditions. When the smoke cleared more than a week later, the fires had burned an astounding 245,000 acres, an area bigger than the state of Indiana. They destroyed 8,900 buildings and killed at least forty-four people.

Zuckerman cheered involuntarily when his house, actually a series of buildings set in a rim of volcanic rocks, came into view—it had survived virtually unscathed. Fire had worked its way around the property, consuming much of the grass and landscaping, including a few stunted blue oaks. It had charred a sliding wood barn door on the outside of the house, which could still be recovered. Burning leaves caught in drain inlets, which are required by code, had discolored the plaster walls in places. But the walls weren't compromised. The fire-prevention strategies employed by Anni Tilt and David Arkin had worked.

The architects created barriers where the landscape meets the house. Plaster protects some walls. Concrete patios block fire from reaching the sides of the house that are cloaked with 1-inch-thick redwood and cedar siding, species that naturally resist fire. Siting the home along the contour of a natural bowl, with rocky terrain rising up around the east, north, and west sides, probably provided additional protection. "The site is amidst some amazing volcanic rock formations, and these may have mitigated some of the winds that were fueling flames the night of the fire," Arkin says.

The most intriguing part of the story is that the home was built with straw—straw

bales covered with a noncombustible lime plaster. It takes two hours for fire to burn through this assembly, according to laboratory tests, compared to less than an hour for most wood-frame structures. "In its baled form, straw is difficult to burn," says Arkin, likening it to a dense telephone book that, if thrown on a fire, would burn slowly. "Plus, there is very little oxygen available to the straw because of the plaster coating. Loose straw will burn, though, and precautions are taken during construction."

A small guesthouse with solar rooftop collectors contains mechanical equipment and a sauna.

Firefighters could draw water from a 27-yard-long lap pool
heated by rooftop solar collectors.

Passive solar techniques result in largely self-regulating interior temperatures. The thick straw-bale walls work with roof overhangs and stained concrete floors to cool the home during summer months. A deep front porch roof facing south provides shade from high summer sun but allows low winter sun to penetrate deep inside, warming the floors and walls. Large sliding doors open to through-breezes that waft up from the valley. On summer evenings, heat that gathers in the tall ceilings gets flushed out through clerestory windows.

Technology kicks in, too. In spring, Rosenberg directs heat from solar hot-water

Straw-bale walls, covered with a lime plaster finish, stayed cool during the wildfire. Salvaged redwood and cedar-panel siding naturally resist fire.

collectors to a 27-yard lap pool. In late fall, she works the system in reverse, closing the windows and using the solar hot water for radiant floor heating. This is usually about the time the solar hot-water heater can't keep up with dropping temperatures in the pool. "This is my favorite job," she says, "turning the heat on and off, marking the change in seasons. I set the radiant heat to 65 in the main house and 63 in the bedrooms and leave it at that for the winter . . . every house should be so easy and efficient."

A 3.5 kW photovoltaic system provides most of the power, feeding excess electricity to the utility grid. The couple pays only about $10 a year for electricity. They harvest drinking water from a 300-foot-deep well on the property—the mountain water is so pure that it doesn't need to be filtered. A pressure tank delivers water to the house and serves fire sprinklers routed through the roof cavity. Firefighters can fill pumper trucks from a standpipe near the driveway.

With its one-story form, rusted corrugated-metal roof, and redwood siding, the stylish home evokes a California ranch vernacular. Porches, patio, and a pool deck connect three

Locally harvested madrone tree-trunk columns support a front porch overhang designed to modulate solar gain.

Sliding doors work in tandem with ceiling fans and clerestory windows to ventilate the home.

main buildings, working their way around boulders. The main building, containing a kitchen, dining room, living room, bathroom, and mudroom, is sited so that corner doors focus attention on beautiful views to the south and southwest.

Straw bale's stellar flame resistance and plastered good looks make it an inspiring example for homeowners in fire-prone regions, especially when other guidelines are followed.

The fire left a repairable pink hue on some plaster walls. The discoloring resulted from leaves that burned in drain inlets. *Photo courtesy of Rosenberg/Zuckerman*

Douglas fir beams and built-in wood shelves balance monolithic plaster surfaces.

ABOVE THE FRAY

Mazama House
Methow Valley, Washington
Finne Architects
4,000 square feet

It's no wonder that Methow Valley in Washington's Cascade Mountains draws year-round weekenders from Seattle. The vacation wonderland, only two hours from Emerald City, has more than 200 kilometers of groomed cross-country ski trails, 120 miles of accessible mountain biking and hiking trails, and class IV river rapids. There's plenty of passive recreation there too. The theater stages productions throughout the year. The gallery screens films. And Winthrop, the re-creation of a gold rush town, even puts on a rodeo.

The region is proving so popular that more and more vacationers are putting down roots and building homes. The influx comes at a time when more-frequent and more-severe droughts have led to record wildfires, most of them caused by people. Architect Nils Finne watched anxiously when reports of the rampaging Carlton Complex wildfire came in from the mountains near the Mazama House he designed for a Seattle couple. The largest fire in Washington State history, it destroyed 353 homes. "We were worried," says Finne. "Thankfully it only got within 25 miles."

The Mazama house, sitting in a copse of trees at the end of a golden meadow, was prepared in case fire reached it. The main living area is raised 7 feet above the field on six

A growing population raises the threat of wildfire in Washington's Methow Valley, a recreational mecca two hours from Seattle. *Photos by Benjamin Benschneider, courtesy of Finne Architects*

Pillars suspend the main living sections 7 feet above a golden meadow. Stone siding protects the wing that touches the ground.

Securely fastened overhangs shelter walkways from frequent
snowfall that can make access to the house difficult.

exposed columns. A bed of crushed stone on the ground serves as a fire-stop. From a distance, the house almost looks like a bridge spanning the meadow. Stone siding protects a bedroom wing that does touch the ground. Flammable plants were kept away from the house's perimeter, and irrigation adds an extra layer of protection.

Fire wasn't Finne's sole environmental concern. The valley also receives 3–4 feet of snow each year, which can make reaching the front door a challenge. A system of deep roof overhangs shelters walkways from snow and rain. A cold roof designed to carry a 100-pound-per-square-foot snow load also prevents icicles from forming, breaking off, and

Meadow grasses are kept away from the house, and a bed of crushed stone serves as a fire-stop.

impaling a passerby. The added benefit of raising the main living areas of the house is that the family can enjoy meadow and mountain views in the winter, when other valley homes are encased in 4-foot snowdrifts. "Many of the homes look bunkered in," Finne says.

The roof overhangs work with concealed interior shades to prevent summer sun from overheating the house. At the same time, broad window walls allow copious sunlight to warm the interior in winter, when the sun is low in the sky. Radiant heat is stored in exposed concrete floors equipped with hydronic heating for cold mountain evenings. Finne gave the house a winter coat of beefed-up insulation—40 percent more than code required—to prevent heat loss. In the summer, high clerestory windows draw hot air out of the house. Water-conserving plumbing fixtures, low-VOC

Serpentine ceiling fixtures unite living areas in a wide-open great room.

Finne either designed or selected the furnishings in the living pavilion, covering sofas and chairs sourced from different designers with the same wool blend.

paints and stains, and locally sourced materials round out the resilient features.

The shade-producing overhangs do at least triple duty. They provide an umbrella of sorts for the owners, Jeff and Nadine Cysewski, to sit outside even during foul weather. And they protect the western red cedar from direct sun exposure. But engineering them—along with the house's defining element, an undulating roof that warps upward at each end—was a daunting challenge. Winds during winter storms routinely reach 60 to 90 miles per hour. "My engineer said, 'this roof wants to sail 50 feet down the road,'" Finne says. He designed a system of hidden hardware connections to prevent just such a disaster.

The Cysewskis, who grew up in Montana, had a short list of requests. Their dream was to own a mountain retreat with a great room featuring a beamed ceiling and large fireplace. A Montana ledgestone fireplace anchors one end of the room, whose undulating roofline,

A fireplace built with Montana ledgestone, one of the homeowner's few requests, anchors the great room.

An eclectic kitchen design features cherry cabinets with a textural band, a custom backsplash from Ann Sacks, and stools with milled-wood tractor seats.

marked by exposed wood beams that fold out like a fan, creates spectacular interior volumes. The beams are supported by unusual steel columns in a tapered "V" shape. They are part of a series of "crafted modernism" details Finne designed that include cast-bronze inserts at the front door, variegated laser-cut steel railing panels, a curvilinear cast-glass kitchen counter, and waterjet-cut aluminum light fixtures.

Finne designed most of the furniture and floor coverings for the great room. He drew on the colors of the meadow, which, thanks to the house and landscape design, keeps its distance in this drought- and fire-prone region.

The kitchen's cherry cabinet pattern reappears in the master bath.

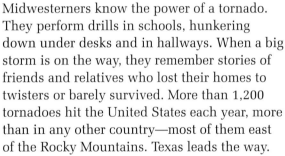

WIND

Midwesterners know the power of a tornado. They perform drills in schools, hunkering down under desks and in hallways. When a big storm is on the way, they remember stories of friends and relatives who lost their homes to twisters or barely survived. More than 1,200 tornadoes hit the United States each year, more than in any other country—most of them east of the Rocky Mountains. Texas leads the way.

People who live by the ocean recount similar storm stories. Each year an average of six hurricanes develop over the Atlantic Ocean, Caribbean Sea, and Gulf of Mexico. Two usually strike the United States, making landfall anywhere from Texas to Maine and taking an average of seventeen lives. People in harm's way become intimately familiar with the storm drill—cover windows and doors, bring patio furniture inside, disconnect

Aycock Moise residence. *Photo courtesy of archimania*

131

electrical appliances, turn off gas and electricity at its source. The best-prepared residents have already elevated outdoor appliances, raised electrical equipment above flood levels, and tied down propane tanks for the grill.

Hurricanes may not be growing more frequent, but they are getting more intense. Scientists tie this development to warming oceans. Since the mid-1970s, the number of hurricanes that reach categories 4 and 5 in strength has roughly doubled. Hurricane Harvey dumped so much rainfall on Texas that the National Weather Service had to add new colors to its rainfall maps. As meteorologists often point out, most hurricane damage comes from flooding after the storm. That was the case with Harvey, which caused an astounding $125 billion in damage, making it the second-most-costly hurricane since 1900.

Winds that exceeded 100 miles per hour did their share of damage too. There isn't much you can do protect a home from a category 4 hurricane or an EF5 tornado. The issue at that level becomes the survival of humans, not buildings. An EF5 tornado with winds over 200 miles per hour can totally destroy even reinforced-concrete structures. But only 2 percent of tornadoes in the United States in any given year reach EF4 or EF5. The reality is that most wind damage is caused by weaker winds on the outskirts of major storms, or lesser storms. Homes can be fortified against most of the fallout from hurricanes and tornados.

A tornado or hurricane, unlike the big bad wolf, doesn't draw air into its lungs and try, with one puff, to blow down an entire building. Instead, it combs the exterior of a building, looking for a weak link. It may enter through a corner incorrectly connected to the roof, a poorly flashed window, or a flimsy garage door on a meager track. Once it finds its way inside, it builds pressure—shaking the house like a soda can—that can blow out windows, doors, walls, and even the roof.

The prescription for limiting damage is similar for both hurricanes and tornadoes. It starts with strapping the roof to the frame and anchoring the frame to the foundation. The house also needs lateral support from high winds that exert outward pressure against sidewalls and upward pressure against the roof. Windows and doors also need to be strong enough to prevent air from getting inside and blowing the house apart.

TORNADO ALLEY

Aycock Moise Residence

Sardis, Mississippi

archimania

4,490 square feet

This durable home, reminiscent of a farmer's shed, is prepared for the next tornado that rips through northern Mississippi. *Photos courtesy of archimania*

Richard Aycock and Claudia Moise were weeks away from moving into their new home when it was demolished by an EF3 tornado. The twister was part of an outbreak of dangerous winds that spread across northern Mississippi and Middle Tennessee, killing thirteen people. Needless to say, the experience changed the couple's perspective when it came time to design a replacement. "The event prompted them to think more about the home's resiliency after a storm," says architect Todd Walker.

The revised version of the couple's dream home contains a centrally located tornado

room built to withstand winds of up to 150 miles per hour. Concrete blocks, reinforced with rebar in every cell, then grouted solid, form the room's walls. They are anchored to the foundation to resist uplift and topped with a concrete ceiling. The concrete assembly is designed to prevent projectiles in an EF3 tornado from penetrating the room. On most days, the chamber houses wine and guns.

The house's main body was designed to battle winds of up to 90 miles per hour. The key to resisting the force of tornadoes—as with earthquakes—is transferring energy from the roof and walls to the ground. Contractors strapped the roof to the walls, anchored the walls to the foundation, and braced the walls with plywood. Structural engineers beefed up

---

Strapping overhangs to walls and anchoring walls to the foundation reduce the likelihood of storm damage.

hardware connections at porch overhangs, corners, and edges, the places where winds accelerate during a storm. The result is a home that's so sturdy it meets California's tough seismic standards.

Sturdy massing and sleek rooflines protect the structure from prevailing south/southwest winds. A solid east-facing wall works with a shed roof to direct driving winds over the top of the building. A guest room and garage facing south block gusts that might otherwise reach the vulnerable covered back porch. Galvanized metal siding and roofing will stand up to driving rain, wind, and fire. The metal cladding reflects the changing colors of the sky and landscape. The house blends into tall pasture grass much like an old barn.

These tactics should help produce the kind of home the couple wants—a simple, durable

A long, open floor plan connects visually to the pool and patio. Windows and doors open to promote cross breezes.

Halfway down the hall, a tornado shelter is engineered to withstand the 130-mile-per-hour winds of an EF3 tornado.

retirement home, a place to escape city life with friends and family. Its long, linear plan means that virtually every interior space opens to the pool and a generous back porch, whose shed roof is sized to shade the interiors from western sun. Doors to the covered porch and windows on the east and west open to promote passive ventilation. Dividing the home into two cooling zones—one in the main living space and bedroom, one for the guest suite—allows for minimal conditioning when the couple is home alone. A backup generator kicks in when utility power goes down.

The house makes a surprising first impression. Visitors arrive at an entry courtyard framed by a screened porch and a carport, and

look up to a hole cut out of the roof. They turn right to the front door and, once inside, look down a long gallery that continues outdoors under the porch. Beyond, a large red sculpture anchors the far end of a lap pool. These polished gestures give the house a transparent quality that belies the building's robust shell.

A solid wall and shed roof direct prevailing winds over the house, protecting the back porch.

A piano fits snugly into a home long on creature comforts, with everything from an exercise studio to a hose-down room for rescue dogs.

HEAVY METAL

Heavy Metal House

Joplin, Missouri

Hufft

5,000 square feet

The Heavy Metal House was armed and ready when a deadly tornado, the third major twister in forty years, touched down in Joplin, Missouri, flattening whole subdivisions, schools, and medical buildings. Owner Bill Perry and his family could take refuge in a windowless shelter built into a crawl space. From there, they could only hope that the house, framed with steel beams and fortified with cold-rolled steel panels, could take what Mother Nature had in store.

The Perrys had left little to chance. Their precautions started with excavation so that the house would be hunkered down below the rest of the lot. The low profile—and a flat roof—would make it difficult for winds to lift the structure. Mature trees were preserved on the 8-acre lot to break high winds, but none were left close enough to topple onto the house. Windows made with tempered glass—two pieces of glass sandwiched around a clear inner layer—could take the brunt of flying debris. A backup generator on a dedicated circuit was ready in case the house lost power. "It will run emergency lights, air if you need it, and the refrigerator," says Dan Brown of Hufft Architects.

Fortified with steel panels and screens, the house survived a catastrophic tornado in Joplin, Missouri, that killed 158 people. *Photos courtesy of Hufft*

Sturdy steel framing was a natural choice for reasons that transcend resiliency. Perry owns a company that uses steel to fabricate commercial scales. Cardinal Detecto also produced 247 perforated steel panels and screens for the exterior. The panels, clipped at the bottom and turned back on the edges, can

be tilted up to clean the windows behind them or admit sunlight to warm the polished concrete floors. Brown varied the perforation patterns to provide visibility in public spaces and privacy in others, and to manage solar gain.

If Perry wanted a fortress, he was also looking for a single-level home with an open flow and views of the 8-acre wooded site. Its long, linear main volume contains a central living and dining area flanked by two wings. One wing contains three secondary bedrooms and a garage. The other, perpendicular to the main volume, contains the master suite, library, and a photography studio with precast concrete walls.

Glass-protective metal panels with calibrated perforations allow light to reach public rooms but keep neighbors from seeing into private spaces.

The living zone's walnut-plank ceiling seems to float above the clerestory windows. Large glass plates and sliding doors allow sunlight to warm the concrete floors and provide unfettered landscape views. Outside, a steel panel serves as a porch screen, blocking unwanted summer sun and shading key interior spots. The walnut planks return in the master suite, where they form a wall between the bedroom and bath.

Long corridors connecting the wings are lined with art and culminate in an outdoor view. The wings wrap around a large, private outdoor courtyard surrounded by dense woods. Most rooms look out to the courtyard or backyard.

The rusting cold-rolled panels and screens make a solid impression during the day. At night, they glow from under-eave lighting that reaches inside the home as well. An illuminated reflecting pool stocked with koi and lilies adds romance to the night scene, while a single can light marks the pivoting walnut front door.

Perry's company also produced gunmetal steel cabinets for the kitchen, steel-clad floors

Screened overhangs fold back to allow daylight to reach the interiors as needed.

A minimalist kitchen with a long concrete countertop and gunmetal-faced casework anchors the large living space.

and walls in the bathrooms, a titan concrete countertop in the kitchen, and a massive walnut dining table. The cabinets were made by covering an MDF (medium-density fiberboard) core with galvanized, hot-rolled steel with a clear-coat finish. No two are exactly alike. Integrated edge pulls give them a minimalist simplicity. Their horizontal shape mirrors the profile of the steel panels and screens outside.

Brown enjoyed collaborating with Perry, who is an attorney and artist in addition to a manufacturer. "The family has this scrappy Midwest mentality. They make everything themselves, even their own computer chips," he says. The pair has created a building that will outlive either party. Throughout the design process, images of Chernobyl kept creeping into Brown's mind's eye. "We wanted to design a building that you could come along to in 500 years and it would still be standing," he says.

River rocks—inside the shower and along glass walls—reinforce the union of interior and exterior spaces.

MOORE, OKLAHOMA, LEADS THE WAY

There's something identifiably different about the new houses going up in Moore, Oklahoma. Nearly all of them, even starter homes, are built with brick or masonry—and on all four sides, an expensive proposition. Monolithic hipped roofs make the homes appear hunkered to the ground. Eaves and overhangs are kept to a minimum.

Moore, part of the Greater Oklahoma City metro region, is one of the few US cities with a tornado code, added after an EF5 tornado with winds of more than 200 miles per hour leveled big swaths of the city. It was the third deadly tornado to hit Moore in fifteen years, and less severe storms also struck during that period.

The differences become even more apparent inside new houses under construction. Hurricane clips (metal plates nailed on two sides) tie rafters to walls. There are more rafters than usual, spaced no more than 16 inches apart. Bolts anchor the foundation to wood base plates. Rigid OSB sheathing

provides lateral support in the walls. Garages are fortified with doors designed to withstand 135-mile-per-hour winds.

New homes are built to withstand the force of an EF3 tornado with winds up to 135 mph, not an EF4 or EF5 tornado, which would destroy everything in its path anyway. When storms reach that level of fierceness, a safe room may be a better investment. Many new homes in Moore, especially on the upper end, also have tornado-safe rooms.

Chris Ramseyer, an associate professor of engineering at the University of Oklahoma in nearby Norman who helped design the Moore code, estimates that the provisions add $1.50 to $2.20 per square foot to the construction cost. That works out to about $3,000 or $4,000 for a 2,000-square-foot house, less than the cost of a granite countertop. Even so, few jurisdictions in Tornado Alley—stretching from North Texas through South Dakota—have followed Moore's lead.

Hurricane clips tie rafters to beams. *Photos by Boyce Thompson*

Bolts anchor walls to foundations.

BUNKER MENTALITY

Prairie Pine Court

Bonita Springs, Florida

Sater Group

3,108 square feet

Dan Sater's Prairie-inspired home survived Hurricane Irma without harm, thanks to a hipped roof, storm-resistant windows, and concrete block construction.
Photos courtesy of Sater Design Collection

Designer Dan Sater vividly remembers the trail of destruction left by Hurricane Andrew, the most massive hurricane ever to hit Florida. The category 5 storm precipitated a new statewide building code to protect new homes from the next big one. Sater decided to exceed the code when it came time to design and build his own house in Bonita Springs. He drew a hipped roof that he knew would be less vulnerable to vicious winds than a gabled roof. He beefed up the strapping that connects roof trusses to walls and topped it off with a metal roof that could better withstand pounding rain and flying debris.

The test came when the National Weather Service warned that Hurricane Irma, the strongest hurricane since Andrew, was on its way. Sater initially intended to ride it out. He moved patio furniture to the garage, unclogged drains, and cleaned debris from the yard. There were no shutters to close—tempered windows on the house render them superfluous. Sater changed his mind at the last moment and drove his family, including his parents, to a second home in the mountains of Georgia. It was a prescient decision—the eye wall of the hurricane came right over the house with winds that reached 130 miles an hour. "Irma hit us hard," he says.

But the house sustained zero damage, except for a few roof tiles that shifted. Trees fell in the yard but didn't reach the house. In fact, damage to homes throughout the area was far less than anticipated, in part because so many were built to the new code. Sater's house lost power but stayed cool even without air conditioning. "With spray foam insulation and low-e windows, the home is actually fairly bearable in summer months. I'm thinking it would make sense, though, to add a backup generator to power the refrigerator, key lights, and other appliances," he says.

Tempered-glass windows eliminated the need for protective shutters. The exterior walls are covered with waterproofing paint.

The Craftsman impression is carried inside with a beamed
ceiling, rolling barn door, and built-in bookshelves.

Like many new homes in Florida, Sater's house is built with concrete block periodically reinforced with rebar and concrete, and is covered on the outside with waterproofing paint. Anchors secure the frame to its foundation, and hurricane straps bond the roof and walls. That way, if wind manages to gets inside through a broken window or vent, it won't blow the roof off, a major problem during Andrew. It doesn't take long for rain to cause major damage inside a decapitated home. Insurers say mold can develop in twenty-four hours.

Florida code also requires beefed-up garage doors, the largest point of potential entry for storm winds. The doors on Sater's three-car garage are reinforced with horizontal steel studs, upgraded springs, a heavy-duty track, heavy-duty rollers, and a beefed-up motor. Virtually every garage door company now offers a hurricane-proof version of its products. Sater didn't have to deal with the possibility of air entering through attic vents. The house didn't need any because spray insulation keeps the attic cool.

The hipped roofline creates a Prairie-style appearance that is reinforced with horizontal fiber-cement siding. Similarly, Craftsman-style elements greet visitors at the front door—stone pilasters and square, tapered columns that support broad, bracketed eaves. The details reappear on a covered porch and veranda in back that nearly double the home's public space. The vaulted veranda contains an outdoor kitchen, fireplace, and conversation pit. Patio doors make it easy for family and party guests to circulate from the great room to the back porch to the veranda.

Inside, tapered columns separate the foyer and formal dining room. Low, built-in bookshelves and wood ceiling beams underscore the Craftsman motif. The plan also caters to the

Concrete construction also results in super-quiet interiors. Here, the large kitchen merges with an eating nook and a veranda.

latest in modern living. Near the garage door, a valet space provides storage for purses, keys, and backpacks, and the utility room includes closets both for storage and hanging clothing to dry. The walk-in pantry serves an island kitchen with built-in seating for four, and a breakfast nook positioned to soak up morning sun opens to the veranda. A foyer marks the entrance to a master suite with his-and-hers closets and vanities, a large walk-in shower, and a linen closet. Each bedroom has its own bath.

Sater incorporates storm resistance features into most of the homes he designs. He markets an entire series of house plans built with concrete. Most are designed for concrete block, but they can be modified to accommodate insulated concrete forms, autoclaved concrete blocks, and poured-in-place concrete wall systems. It may cost more to build with concrete than with wood. But concrete offers key advantages: soundproofing, fireproofing, and of course structural stability in the event of big storms.

Fortified garage doors protect the house and Sater's car collection from hurricane winds.

INVESTIGATORS TRACK DAMAGE IN DALLAS

After at least twelve tornadoes ripped through the Dallas suburbs in December 2015, including one that reached EF4, forensic engineers from the American Plywood Association swooped in to investigate. It was hard for them to learn anything from homes directly in the path of the strongest winds; they were flattened. The team focused instead on homes beat up by winds from smaller, less violent tornadoes. They "produce winds which a carefully constructed building can be expected to withstand," reported the APA (https://royomartin.com, 2015).

The houses that didn't hold up had been poorly built. Most damage was due to improper connections between roof and walls. Framers had merely driven toenails through roof framing into the top plate of the exterior walls. Inexpensive light-gauge metal connectors could have saved many of the roofs, according to the engineers. "With these, the load is resisted in directions perpendicular to the nail shank rather than acting to pull the nail straight out. Use of

---

Newly built homes failed when relatively mild tornadoes ripped through the Dallas suburbs. Inspectors determined that walls had been poorly braced and brick veneer had been improperly installed. *Photos courtesy of APA, Engineered Wood Association*

these metal connectors was only observed in one case among the homes where loss of the roof structure occurred."

Another common, very preventable cause of failure: using pins instead of anchor bolts to attach walls to the foundation. In most cases, framers shot pins from nail guns to attach the bottom of support walls to concrete-slab foundations. The technique saves time and money and meets many local building codes. But most modern building codes, the report says, call for "deformed steel anchor bolts to be embedded into reinforced concrete foundations for attachment of wood framing."

Other buildings crumbled because of weak walls without lateral bracing; they were sheathed with ⅛-inch laminated fiberboard rather than thicker OSB or plywood. Investigators found that the thin sheathing didn't transfer framing loads within wall systems, especially at corners and between floors.

Poorly installed brick veneer wall cladding created other hazards. "Falling brick from veneered walls, columns, and chimneys was observed across a wide range of wind speeds in the impacted areas, representing a considerable threat to life safety," the report stated.

Many homes blew apart due to the failure of windows, garage doors, and exterior cladding. Even in areas with low to moderate wind speeds, holes allowed air to get inside and pressurize the building interior. That exacerbated load path deficiencies, with catastrophic results.

Framers had used nail guns, rather than beefed-up connectors, to build roof assemblies.

Diagram courtesy of APA, Engineered Wood Association

FIGURE 1

TIPS FOR IMPROVING TORNADO RESISTANCE OF LIGHT-FRAME WOOD CONSTRUCTION

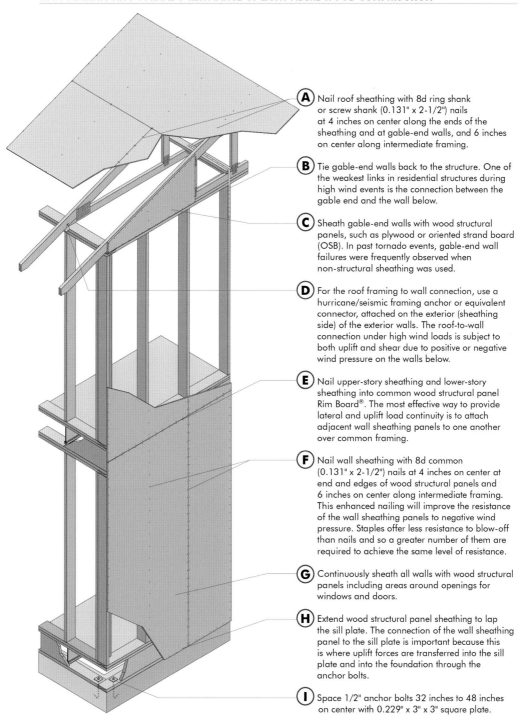

(A) Nail roof sheathing with 8d ring shank or screw shank (0.131" x 2-1/2") nails at 4 inches on center along the ends of the sheathing and at gable-end walls, and 6 inches on center along intermediate framing.

(B) Tie gable-end walls back to the structure. One of the weakest links in residential structures during high wind events is the connection between the gable end and the wall below.

(C) Sheath gable-end walls with wood structural panels, such as plywood or oriented strand board (OSB). In past tornado events, gable-end wall failures were frequently observed when non-structural sheathing was used.

(D) For the roof framing to wall connection, use a hurricane/seismic framing anchor or equivalent connector, attached on the exterior (sheathing side) of the exterior walls. The roof-to-wall connection under high wind loads is subject to both uplift and shear due to positive or negative wind pressure on the walls below.

(E) Nail upper-story sheathing and lower-story sheathing into common wood structural panel Rim Board®. The most effective way to provide lateral and uplift load continuity is to attach adjacent wall sheathing panels to one another over common framing.

(F) Nail wall sheathing with 8d common (0.131" x 2-1/2") nails at 4 inches on center at end and edges of wood structural panels and 6 inches on center along intermediate framing. This enhanced nailing will improve the resistance of the wall sheathing panels to negative wind pressure. Staples offer less resistance to blow-off than nails and so a greater number of them are required to achieve the same level of resistance.

(G) Continuously sheath all walls with wood structural panels including areas around openings for windows and doors.

(H) Extend wood structural panel sheathing to lap the sill plate. The connection of the wall sheathing panel to the sill plate is important because this is where uplift forces are transferred into the sill plate and into the foundation through the anchor bolts.

(I) Space 1/2" anchor bolts 32 inches to 48 inches on center with 0.229" x 3" x 3" square plate.

GALLERY ROW

Artery House

Kansas City, Missouri

Hufft

10,650 square feet

When tornadoes threaten their Kansas City home, Christy and Bill Gautreaux and their two daughters can hunker down in, of all places, an art gallery. That's right—the concrete-walled, sublevel art gallery in their home includes a tornado-safe room that's used for art storage on most days. Odds are that when they emerge from the tornado shelter, damage to the rest of the house will be minimal. The upper floors are framed with steel, and windows are made with tempered glass. If utility power goes out, a standby generator runs the heating system, select lights, refrigeration, and appliances.

Depending on the season, the Gautreauxes may not need much utility support. Passive and active solar tactics allow the Prairie-style home to nearly stand on its own. Large south-facing overhangs shield summer sun even as they invite winter sun to heat thermal masses—a stone floor and limestone interior walls. A 21.5 kW photovoltaic array covering the main wing can power the entire house except in late fall and winter, when the family could return to pioneer days

Artery House's owners can take refuge in the concrete-walled subterranean art gallery fitted with a tornado-safe room. A permeable driveway slopes to a trench drain that prevents sheets of stormwater from reaching the house. *Photos by Michael Robinson*

The main entry highlights the Prairie-style home's locally sourced limestone, cedar, and stainless steel.

and throw some wood on a three-story stone fireplace. "The family can live comfortably in a power outage," says architect Matthew Hufft, whose firm not only designed the home and its interiors but built it, along with most of the interior casework, hardware, and furniture.

These resiliencies protect a world-class art collection. Viewings start in the gallery, lit with natural and LED lighting, and extend through a three-story central artery of hallways and vertical atriums. Soft, indirect lighting accents installations along movable walls. A sculpture park with grass pavers extends the collection into the landscape. The gallery can have its own entrance because the home is on a corner lot. "The arrangement allows the homeowners

to share their amazing art collection with the public, without having them in their actual house," says Hufft.

The house itself is a work of art, especially from a resiliency perspective. The program of self-reliance starts with a rainscreen—a slight gap behind the building envelope and exterior cladding to channel away water before it gets inside the wall. A composite "cool" roof resists ultraviolet light and ozone. A permeable driveway—formed by a series of large pavers—slopes to a trench drain that prevents sheets of water from reaching the house. A wall of sliding patio doors on the first floor works with clerestory windows on the upper levels to naturally ventilate the house.

Light from an open stairwell reaches into a long gallery generous enough to display large paintings and photographs.

M. C. Escher's *Relativity* inspired the design for a floating steel-and-walnut staircase.

Refined interior details—walnut cabinets, custom metal hardware, and an LED light fixture with 300 programmable pendants, belie the home's extreme resiliency.

A wall of south-facing windows reinforced with tempered glass runs the length of the main wing.

A wall of tempered, double-paned mahogany windows and patio doors fills the public spaces with natural light, minimizing the use of electricity during the day. Dark limestone, the same material used on the exterior, clads a fireplace with an off-center firebox. It anchors a low-slung family room that merges with a long porch. The main level contains the living room, kitchen, dining room, and his-and-her offices. Five upper-level bedrooms—for the couple, their two children, and two lucky guests—take the form of cedar-wrapped boxes, with expansive windows screened by aluminum louvers.

The minimalist kitchen is where Hufft's interior work really sings. The firm designed and built the kitchen hardware using a 3-D printer that works with stainless steel. Cabinets are made from walnut with two different stains, the darker color syncing with the window frames and limestone. Hufft also designed and fabricated much of the casework and furniture, including the tables, media center, and master bed. Many of the pieces feature knife-edge detailing inspired by the home's dramatic overhangs. As refined as they are, though, these interior elements play second fiddle to the rigor of a structure built with extreme weather in mind.

The house wraps around a tension-edge swimming pool. Native grasses soften virtually tornado-proof concrete walls.

RESILIENT DESIGN
FOCUSES ON PREVENTING
THE LION'S SHARE OF
DISASTER DAMAGE.

A guest suite secured with steel trusses cantilevers dramatically over the courtyard.

RESOURCES

WATER

Building Science Corporation periodically publishes valuable guidance for designing new homes to resist natural disasters. "BSI-101: Rebuilding Houston," by Joseph Lstiburek, PhD, details methods first published after Hurricane Katrina for designing homes to resist flooding. www.buildingscience.com.

Disastersafety.org, an online portal created by insurers, publishes useful technical bulletins that outline protections from hurricanes and tornadoes. Its 128-page "Hurricane Standards" is referenced by some local building departments. www.disastersafety.org.

FEMA publishes a guide to product specifications, including interior finishes, for houses in flood-prone regions: "Flood Damage–Resistant Materials Requirements." Technical Bulletin 2, August 2008. www.fema.gov.

One of the best resources for flood-hardy construction is the LaHouse Resource Center, run by **Louisiana State University's Ag Center**. Check out "The Flood-Hardy Wall." An FAQ section of the website provides new-construction tips. www.lsuagcenter.com.

New York State publishes a wonderfully illustrated *Build Better Guide* available in print and online. Drawings show the correct waterproof installation of windows, roofing, vents, and other building systems. www.nyserda.ny.gov.

FIRE

FEMA publishes "Defensible Space," a home builder's guide to construction in wildfire zones that also provides landscaping guidance. It describes how to establish zones that keep flammable vegetation away from the house. www.fema.gov.

International Code Council publishes the International Wildland-Urban Interface Code, referenced by state and local building codes. The code provides guidance for building materials, systems, and landscaping that will stand up to wildfire. https://codes.iccsafe.org.

National Fire Protection Association runs a Firewise USA program that includes voluntary guidelines for fire-safe design and construction. The program includes recommendations for living with the threat of wildfire and working with neighbors on prevention measures. The organization also publishes a series of tip sheets for preventing fire from starting inside the home. www.nfpa.org.

EARTH

APA (American Plywood Association) publishes a handy "Introduction to Lateral Design" that explains how wood-framed houses respond to the lateral forces of earthquakes and high winds. www.apawood.org.

California Seismic Safety Commission's "The Homeowner's Guide to Earthquake Safety" identifies weak spots in a home during an earthquake, such as unsecured water heaters and walls that aren't anchored to a foundation. https://ssc.ca.gov.

"Damage to Foundations from Expansive Soils," by J. David Rogers, Robert Olshansky, and Robert B. Roberts, explains the threat to foundations from swelling clays. www.researchgate.net.

FEMA publishes the "Homebuilder's Guide to Earthquake Resistant Design and Construction," a guide to the best current practices. It's based on lessons learned from major US earthquakes. www.fema.gov.

Hardware manufacturer **Simpson Strong-Tie** publishes "A Step-by-Step Guide to Retrofit Your Home for Earthquakes" that outlines steps to reinforce a house's structural frame. http://mitigation.eeri.org.

WIND

Disastersafety.org publishes "Hurricane Standards," a guide to hurricane-safe construction. It focuses on reducing dangers from roof uplift, attic ventilation, windows, and garage doors, among other things. www.disastersafety.org.

FEMA's 184-page "Home Builder's Guide to Coastal Construction" rolls up several homeowner-friendly fact sheets into one document. Building a house that can stand up to a hurricane requires attention to small details that can sometimes fall through the cracks. www.fema.gov.

Hawaii's Department of Commerce and Consumer Affairs publishes the "Guide to Hurricane Strengthening for Hawaii Single-Family Residences." It provides an overview of how to protect homes from strong wind forces. https://cca.hawaii.gov.

Moore, Oklahoma, is one of the nation's few cities with tornado provisions in its building code, "Moore Oklahoma Building Code." It also publishes a two-page checklist for new construction and retrofits. https://library.municode.com.

ARCHITECTS &

ARTERY HOUSE
Architect and builder: Hufft, Kansas City, Missouri, hufft.com

AYCOCK MOISE RESIDENCE
Architect: archimania, Memphis, Tennessee, archimania.com
Builder: Oak River Fine Homes, Memphis, Tennessee

BEACH HAVEN RESIDENCE
Architect: Specht Architects, Austin, New York, spechtarchitects.com
Builder: Demmerle Builders, West Creek, New Jersey, facebook/demmerlebuilders

FALL HOUSE
Architect: Fougeron Architecture, San Francisco, fougeron.com/
Builder: Thomas George Construction, Carmel, California, gosmith.com/pro/1285551

HEAVY METAL HOUSE
Architect: Hufft, Kansas City, Missouri, hufft.com
Builder: Harry Young, Joplin, Missouri

HIBISCUS ISLAND HOUSE
Architect: Cheoff Levy Fischman, Miami, clfarchitects.com
Builder: Bosch Construction and Eddie Irvine, Miami Beach, boschconstruction.net

MAZAMA HOUSE
Architect: Finne Architects, Seattle, finne.com
Builder: Rick Mills, North Cascades Construction, Winthrop, Washington, ncc-methow.com/contact.html

PRAIRIE PINE COURT
Designer and builder: Sater Group, Bonita Springs, Florida, satergroup.com

ROSENBERG-ZUCKERMAN RESIDENCE
Architect: Arkin Tilt Architects, Berkeley, California, arkintilt.com
Builder: Fault-Line Builders, Sonoma Hills, California, faultlinebuilders.com

SARATOGA HILL HOUSE
Architect: Designs Northwest Architects, Seattle, designsnw.com
Builder: Waite Construction, Camano Island, Washington, islandcountycontractors.com

BUILDERS

SOUTH FIFTH STREET
Architect: Alterstudio, Austin, Texas,
alterstudio.net
Builder: Anne Suttles and Sam Shah,
Austin, Texas

TEABERRY
Architect: Cary Bernstein Architect, San
Francisco, cbstudio.com
Builder: Weitekamp Remodeling &
Construction, Antioch, California, wremodel-
ing.com

TROLLEY HOUSE
Architect: Beinfield Architecture, South
Norwalk, Connecticut, beinfield.com
Builder: RDC Construction, Stamford,
Connecticut

TSUNAMI HOUSE
Architect: Designs Northwest Architects,
Seattle, designsnw.com
Builder: JP Land Builder, Camano Island,
Washington, jplandbuilder.com

WYOMING RESIDENCE
Architect: Abramson Teiger Architects, Culver
City, California, abramsonteiger.com
Builder: Dynamic Custom Homes, Jackson,
Wyoming, dchjh.com

ZEN HACIENDA HOUSE
Architect: DMHA Architecture, Santa Barbara,
California, dmhaa.com
Builder: Gene Vernon, Solvang, California

Boyce Thompson

is the author of *Anatomy of a Great Home*
and *The New New Home*. The former editor of
Builder magazine and founding editor of
Residential Architect magazine, Thompson has
spent more than 30 years writing about home
design and construction.